The Texan Army, 1835–46

Stuart Reid • Illustrated by Richard Hook

Series editor Martin Windrow

First published in Great Britain in 2003 by Osprey Publishing
Elms Court, Chapel Way, Botley, Oxford OX2 9LP, United Kingdom.
Email: **info@ospreypublishing.com**

ISBN 1 84176 593 7

Editor: Martin Windrow
Design: Alan Hamp
Index by Alan Rutter
Maps by Stuart Reid
Originated by Electronic Page Company, Cwmbran, UK
Printed in China through World Print Ltd.

03 04 05 06 07   10 9 8 7 6 5 4 3 2 1

FOR A CATALOGUE OF ALL BOOKS PUBLISHED BY
OSPREY MILITARY AND AVIATION PLEASE CONTACT:

The Marketing Manager, Osprey Direct UK
PO Box 140, Wellingborough, Northants,
NN8 2FA, United Kingdom
Email: **info@ospreydirect.co.uk**

The Marketing Manager, Osprey Direct USA
c/o MBI Publishing
729 Prospect Avenue, Osceola, WI 54020, USA
Email: **info@ospreydirectusa.com**

www.ospreypublishing.com

09498525

Dedication

To the memory of Colonel James Grant, killed at Agua Dulce Creek, 2 March 1836; 'a scholar, gentleman and soldier.'

Editor's Note

In series style, this text on an American subject mainly employs standard US conventions of spelling and punctuation. However, the inclusion of contemporary quoted passages makes some inconsistencies inevitable, e.g. in the different spellings of "grey/gray" favored at different periods. The contemporary term "Texian" is also used.

Artist's Note

Readers may care to note that the original paintings from which the color plates in this book were prepared are available for private sale. All reproduction copyright whatsoever is retained by the Publishers. All enquiries should be addressed to:

Scorpio Gallery, PO Box 475, Hailsham, E.Sussex BN27 2SL

The Publishers regret that they can enter into no correspondence upon this matter.

THE TEXAN ARMY 1835–46

INTRODUCTION

ACCORDING TO "BIG FOOT" WALLACE, they were a "motley, mixed up crowd, you may be certain – broken down politicians from the 'old States' that somehow had got on the wrong side of the fence, and had been left out in the cold; renegades and refugees from justice, that had 'left their country for their country's good,' and adventurers of all sorts, ready for anything or any enterprise that afforded a reasonable prospect of excitement and plunder. Dare-devils they were all, and afraid of nothing under the sun (except perhaps a due-bill or a bailiff)."

They were also, overwhelmingly, Americans; and therein lay the key to the story. Texas was originally a thinly populated province of Mexico forming part of the federal state of Coahuila y Tejas. While the massive influx of American settlers into the region begun by Stephen Austin in the 1820s and 1830s ultimately made conflict inevitable, the Texan Revolution was also part of a much wider Mexican civil war between the conservative *Centralistas* or *Santanistas* and the liberal *Federalistas*.

The country's US-inspired 1824 constitution, which allowed considerable autonomy to the Mexican states, had been annulled after General Antonio Lopez de Santa Anna seized power in 1834; and over the next decade a series of poorly co-ordinated federalist and secessionist revolts broke out against his rule, as far apart as Yucatan and New Mexico.

In Texas the situation was aggravated by ethnic and cultural differences. In order to encourage settlement the Mexican authorities had originally offered a number of attractive concessions, which effectively amounted to an absence of government and ultimately worked against the assimilation of the colonists into Mexican society. Moreover, for some time there had been pressure from the colonists for Texas to be separated from Coahuila and recognized as a federal state in its own right; but thus far such recognition had been resisted by the central government, through a well-founded fear that it would merely be the prelude to eventual American annexation. Consequently American immigration had officially been suspended by the Mexican government for that very reason in 1830. Predictably this aroused considerable resentment,

General Sam Houston (1793–1863) as depicted in an 1838 lithograph. This single-breasted uniform with a lone star on the collar appears in a number of contemporary portraits, but is not described in the 1839 regulations. (Texas State Library and Archives Commission)

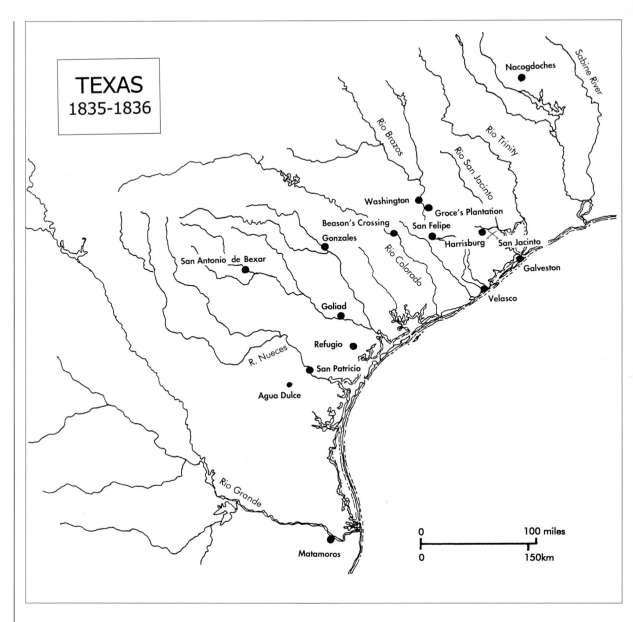

since the overwhelming majority of the incomers still thought of themselves as Americans and behaved accordingly, particularly when the Mexican central government threatened to become more oppressive than the US one which they had left. Notwithstanding, many "Texians" initially rejected calls for a declaration of independence; instead, they and their *Tejano* neighbours at first took up arms with the professed intention of upholding the Mexican Federalist constitution of 1824 and its supposed guarantees of their democratic rights.

Thus, when General Martin Perfecto de Cos landed in Texas with the intention of disarming its unruly citizens and putting a final end to American immigration, he instead found himself facing a full-blown rebellion which was rapidly to turn into a revolution – and which ultimately led to the United States reaching the Pacific Ocean.

OPPOSITE **In 1835 the southern boundary between Texas and the neighboring state of Tamaulipas was the Rio Nueces, not the Rio Grande – the lower part of which was also confusingly known as the Rio Bravo. The inhospitable prairie between the two rivers was to be disputed territory until the international border was finally fixed on the Rio Grande after the American-Mexican War of 1846–48. Note that during the Revolution, San Antonio de Bexar was known simply as Bexar, though it later became San Antonio. Goliad was better known at the time as La Bahia.**

CHRONOLOGY

1835
30 June Texian insurgents attack Anahuac
13 July Uprising in Nacogdoches
2 October Battle of Gonzales
28 October Battle of Concepcion
5–9 December Storming of San Antonio de Bexar
1836
1 January James Grant leads Federal Volunteer Army out of Bexar
16 February Santa Anna crosses Rio Grande
23 February Siege of Alamo begins
27 February Battle of San Patricio
2 March Texan declaration of independence; battle of Agua Dulce
6 March Alamo stormed by Mexican Army
19 March Battle of Coleto Creek
27 March Goliad massacre
21 April Battle of San Jacinto
4 July United States recognizes Republic of Texas
22 October Sam Houston inaugurated as first president of Republic
1840
15 March "Council House Fight" at San Antonio de Bexar
12 August Battle of Plum Creek
1841
19 June Santa Fe expedition departs Kenney's Fort
5 October Texians surrender at Laguno Colorado near Santa Fe
1842
5–7 March Vazquez's raid on San Antonio de Bexar
11–19 September Woll's raid on San Antonio de Bexar
17 September Battle of Salado Creek
22 September Battle of Arroyo Hondo
8 December Somervell expedition captures Laredo
26 December Battle of Mier
1843
24 April Snively expedition departs Georgetown
20 June Battle of Crooked Creek, New Mexico

1844
22 April Treaty of Annexation with United States
1845
25 July American "Corps of Observation" arrives at Corpus Christi, Texas
29 December State of Texas admitted to Union
1846
19 February Formal transfer of sovereignty to United States
13 May United States declares war on Mexico

Captain Andrew Robinson's Harrisburg Volunteers carried this red, white and blue tricolor with a white star next to the staff at the siege of Bexar. Creed Taylor states that it was afterwards left in the Alamo "and that fragments... were found in the ruins after the fall of the fortress."

5

THE REVOLUTION

After a promising start the 1835 Texian insurrection against Santa Anna's government stagnated. In the open – as they clearly demonstrated at Gonzales and Concepcion – the Texians' rifles were deadly; but, secure inside San Antonio de Bexar, General Cos could afford to wait while the rebels quarreled amongst themselves and drifted homewards in ever growing numbers. By the beginning of December the rebel leaders were ready to abandon the siege entirely and retire eastwards across the Guadalupe river. Then, in one of history's more dramatic turningpoints, a trio of "filibusters" – Ben Milam, Frank Johnson and Dr James Grant – prevented the retreat by engineering and then leading an all-out assault on the town.[1] Grant was wounded at the outset and Milam was killed on the third day of the battle, but the attack achieved its purpose. Cos surrendered on 9 December, and enough of the Texian army afterwards remained in being to join Grant's proposed expedition to Matamoros, down on the Rio Grande.

As far back as 5 November, Stephen Austin himself had declared that "Nothing will aid Texas as much as an expedition against Matamoros under General Mexia – it is all important." Instead, Mexia, with a motley collection of largely American mercenaries, had tried unsuccessfully to seize Tampico further down the coast; but on 17 December the Texian General Council at San Felipe de Austin resolved on another attempt. This was intended to encourage a Federalist insurrection in Tamaulipas and, by so carrying the war into the interior, to disrupt or even prevent Santa Anna's imminent invasion of Texas.

The Texian nemesis: General Antonio Lopez de Santa Anna Pérez de Lebrón (1794–1876). A shameless political opportunist who changed sides several times during his career, Santa Anna was brutal, capricious, and – although capable of a headstrong energy that sometimes brought him success – a commander of strictly limited talents.

Agua Dulce, the Alamo, Goliad and San Jacinto

Sam Houston was accordingly ordered to set it in motion; but he dragged his heels, and on 1 January 1836 it was Grant's "Federal Volunteer Army" that marched from Bexar – with the aim of joining with the *Federalistas* in establishing a new Republic of Northern Mexico. Two weeks later, after a memorable falling out between the Council and the provisional governor, Henry Smith, Sam Houston caught up with the army at Goliad and succeeded in wrecking the expedition by persuading a substantial number of men to remain in Texas as auxiliary volunteers. None of them would recognize his authority, however; so, leaving them at Refugio to await the arrival of the

---

1 Though today it has a specialized political meaning, in the early 19th century "filibuster" – through the Spanish *filibustero,* from older French and Dutch terms – meant simply a piratical adventurer or freebooter.

Council's agent, Colonel James Fannin, Houston took himself off to visit his Cherokee friends in East Texas.

Undaunted, Grant still pressed on with just 64 men to the then Texas border on the River Nueces at San Patricio. From there he led a series of raids into the Rio Grande valley with the dual aim of establishing contact with the curiously elusive *Federalistas*, and of rounding up sufficient horses and mules to mount all of Fannin's men once they arrived. In the meantime a Mexican army led by Santa Anna swept into Texas, and the complexion of the war changed. In the face of this clear and present danger the Texians put aside their differences and defiantly proclaimed their independence from Mexico – only to face a succession of disasters.

While returning from one of their forays on 2 March – the day that Texian independence was formally declared at San Felipe – Grant and his men were ambushed and killed at Agua Dulce. By this time the irresolute Fannin, far from advancing to his aid, had fallen back from Refugio to Goliad, from where he had launched an abortive attempt to reach the Alamo garrison in Bexar, besieged by Santa Anna since 23 February.

Two days after the declaration of independence Sam Houston was confirmed as major-general and finally given authority over all the volunteer troops as well as his handful of regulars; but – no doubt recognizing the futility of marching against Santa Anna – he made no attempt to save the Alamo, which was stormed on 6 March[2]. Instead he avowedly planned to defend the line of the Colorado river, and summoned Fannin to join him there at Beason's Crossing. However, the latter once again demonstrated his incapacity by lingering too long at Goliad, and was intercepted and forced to surrender on the open prairie near Coleto Creek on 20 March. A week later he and his men were marched out and shot down in cold blood.

With insufficient men to hold the line of the Colorado, Houston and the remaining Texians then fled eastwards in a headlong retreat afterwards ruefully celebrated as the "runaway scrape." His intention was simply to run for the border "and the old flag," perhaps in the hope of triggering US intervention; but in the event his men forced him to make a stand at San Jacinto, where they won an unexpected victory over Santa Anna on 21 April. The Generalissimo himself was among the prisoners, and agreed to order all Mexican forces to evacuate Texas. However, while the Treaty of Velasco ostensibly ended overt hostilities, Mexico refused to recognize Texas as an independent state, and fighting continued sporadically for the next ten years.

The state flag of Coahuila y Texas, possibly carried by Benavides' or Seguin's *Federalistas* at the siege of Bexar, and – according to at least two Mexican accounts – subsequently flown at the outset of the defense of the Alamo, rather than the 1824 flag. Like the latter it was a green/white/ red tricolor, and as one gold star represented Coahuila and the other Texas, it is likely that this is the origin of the 'lone star' for Texas alone.

THE REPUBLIC

After the battle of San Jacinto, Sam Houston turned over command of the army to Thomas Jefferson Rusk and went to New Orleans for treatment to his ankle, which had been badly shattered by a canister round. In his absence another raid was planned on Matamoros after two Texian commissioners were arrested there in July while negotiating an exchange of prisoners. Although the port was blockaded by the Texian Navy, nothing came of the expedition and the proposal was abandoned after Sam Houston returned, to become president of the new Republic on 22 October. With his inauguration, Rusk's caretaker role came to an

In the 1830s the northern boundaries of Texas and some of the other Mexican states were very vaguely defined, if at all, leading to considerable conflict in later years.

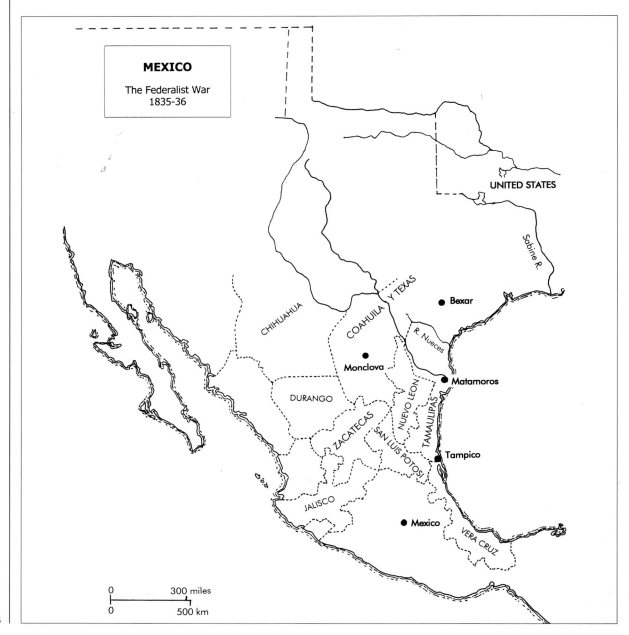

MEXICO

The Federalist War
1835-36

UNITED STATES

Sabine R.

CHIHUAHUA

COAHUILA Y TEXAS

● Bexar

R. Nueces

● Monclova

● Matamoros

DURANGO

NUEVO LEON

ZACATECAS

SAN LUIS POTOSI

TAMAULIPAS

● Tampico

JALISCO

● Mexico

VERA CRUZ

0   300 miles
0   500 km

end and day-to-day command of the army then passed to the decidedly unstable Brigadier-General Felix Huston.

This soon turned out to be a mistake. Huston, a "turbulent and overbearing" Mississippi planter, had no previous military experience and was a poor disciplinarian. Consequently, in December 1836 a West Point graduate named Albert Sidney Johnston became the senior brigadier.[3] Outraged, Huston declared Johnston's appointment to be an attempt "to ruin my reputation and inflict a stigma on my character," and promptly challenged him to a duel. After no fewer than three shots had been exchanged by both parties, he put a bullet into Johnston's right hip. This rather unconventional promotion gambit was to no effect, however, and as soon as he was able Johnston began cracking down hard on the disciplinary problems inherited from his murderous predecessor.

Unfortunately a combination of boredom (scarcely alleviated by intensive drill), short and monotonous rations, poor clothing and an over-abundant supply of worse whisky led to rampant insubordination which occasionally turned into violent acts of mutiny. The officers were just as quarrelsome, and in the nine years which followed the battle of San Jacinto the Texian Army would actually lose more officers killed by their own colleagues than by the Mexican Army and the Comanches together.

Mirabeau Buonaparte Lamar (1798–1895). Born in Louisville, Georgia, Lamar was given a verbal commission as colonel of cavalry at San Jacinto, and within a month was named major-general – only to be rejected by the rank and file. However, as president of the Republic he strengthened the regular army and embarked on an ultimately unsuccessful policy of expansion. After annexation by the USA he served under Zachary Taylor as an officer in the Texas Mounted Volunteers. (Texas State Library and Archives Commission)

Disgusted, still suffering from his poorly healed wound and at odds with President Houston, A.S.Johnston resigned, and on 7 May 1837 turned over temporary command to Colonel Joseph Rogers, the senior officer at headquarters. Aware that Felix Huston and others were still agitating for another raid on Matamoros, the president defused both issues by sending two-thirds of the army on furlough, retaining only about 500 men to garrison the most essential posts. By the end of that year only the small garrisons of regulars at San Antonio de Bexar and Galveston remained.

Lamar's presidency

However, after Mirabeau Buonaparte Lamar succeeded Houston as president on 10 December 1838, the regular army was dramatically revived. Lamar shared James Grant's old vision of a greater Texas embracing the other northern Mexican states to stretch all the way from the Gulf to the Pacific. Moreover, while Sam Houston had enjoyed good relations with the Cherokees and other Native American tribes in East Texas, Lamar was firmly of the opinion that they were occupying far too much valuable land – an important consideration for a state whose only resource was its land, whether to pay its soldiers and other creditors or to underwrite foreign loans. Conflict was inevitable, and for that Lamar needed a real army.

3 See Elite 94, *American Civil War Commanders (4) Confederate Leaders in the West*

On the recommendation of the new secretary of war – Albert Sidney Johnston – all the remaining regulars were consolidated into a new "Frontier Regiment," which although including both a cavalry and an ordnance element continued to be referred to as the 1st Regiment of Infantry. Ostensibly its purpose was to garrison a string of forts along a military road to be constructed along the northern and western frontier from the Red River to the Nueces. Although a brave start was made and some of the forts were constructed, the road was never completed, and few of the required additional recruits ever materialized. Consequently, while some regulars fought in the Cherokee War, in the celebrated "Council House Fight" with the Comanches at San Antonio (when a peace conference went disastrously wrong), and at the subsequent battle of Plum Creek, most of the Indian fighting and border defense continued to be undertaken by volunteer Ranger companies and militia.

The Alamo chapel shortly before its acquisition by the US Army in 1850 and the subsequent "restoration"; it was already a potent shrine to Texan independence. Although the scale is dramatically exaggerated, this engraving closely resembles a daguerreotype made in the late 1840s which came to light during the 1990s.

1839: Canales and the "Republic of Rio Grande"

Meanwhile, Lamar was not the only one to revive the idea of a Republic of Northern Mexico. On the other side of the Nueces, Antonio Canales, who had been one of James Grant's *Federalista* contacts during the revolution, again invoked the constitution of 1824, and in September 1839 led yet another uprising against the *Centralistas*. Proclaiming the independent Republic of Rio Grande, which was to encompass the northern Mexican states of Tamaulipas, Nuevo Leon and Coahuila, Canales appealed to Texas for aid and laid siege to Matamoros. Although Lamar declined to become directly involved (officially, at least), he did nothing to discourage Canales from recruiting mercenaries and filibusters for a "Texian Auxiliary Corps."

OPPOSITE **This simple flag bearing a gold star on a blue field, designed by David G.Burnet, served as the national flag of the Republic of Texas from about December 1836 until replaced by the much more familiar Lone Star flag in 1839.**

Antonio Canales (1802–52) was a Mexican *Federalista* who initially promised to co-operate with James Grant's filibusters during the Revolution, but got cold feet when the Texians declared inependence. He later enlisted Texian aid for his would-be Republic of Rio Grande, but betrayed the Texian Auxiliary Corps when he and his supporters changed sides. Intriguingly, his subsequent border raiding earned him the nickname of the "Chapparal Fox" – *El Zorro.*

It was probably going a little too far, however, when a newly raised Gonzales Ranging Company led by Captain Reuben Ross signed up en masse for the promise of 25 dollars a month, and disappeared south of the border with an unspecified quantity of "public property" including a Texas flag. Worse still, the following August the second-in-command of the reorganized 1st Regiment of Infantry, Lieutenant-Colonel William Fisher, also enlisted in Canales' cause and marched off from San Antonio with about 200 men. He was followed a little later by another 100 or so under Captain Samuel Jordan, late of the 1st Cavalry, and 200 *Tejanos* led by Lieutenant-Colonel Juan Seguin, late of the short-lived 2nd Cavalry.

Just when matters appeared to be getting out of hand, Canales' would-be Republic of Rio Grande collapsed. There were ominous warning signs when the siege of Matamoros was abandoned, and it became apparent that none of the promised pay was going to be forthcoming. Canales also began objecting to that Texas flag. Then, one morning as *Centralistas* and *Federalistas* seemingly lined up to fight at Ojo del Agua near Saltillo, Canales and his men suddenly went over to the other side. The bewildered Texian mercenaries beat a hasty retreat to a nearby hacienda and held off the Mexicans until nightfall, before making a run for the Rio Grande. From then onwards Canales was a marked man so far as the Texians were concerned.

Unfortunately this affair had other lasting repercussions. Seguin extricated his own men from the débâcle at Ojo del Agua and got them across the Rio Grande so promptly as to raise shrewd suspicions that he had some foreknowledge of Canales' treachery, and eventually this veteran of the Alamo and San Jacinto found it expedient to abandon Texas. Next time he came back to San Antonio it would be as a Mexican soldier.

The 1841 Santa Fe expedition

In the meantime, despite Lamar's argument that the regular army's value lay not in "its actual fighting" but as a deterrent, the fifth Congress adjourned on 5 February 1841 without appropriating any funds to extend the soldiers' three-year enlistments, which were due to expire that August. This setback did nothing to restrain Lamar's expansionist policies and, in defiance of Houston and his supporters, a military expedition was despatched to Santa Fe in neighboring New Mexico. It was naked filibustering. Ostensibly the expedition's purpose was to open up a trade route, but the merchants who left Kenney's Fort on 19 June were escorted by no fewer than 270 well-clothed and equipped (if soon to be

George B.Crittenden (1812–80). A native of Kentucky and graduate of West Point, Crittenden served in the Black Hawk War before going to Texas and participating in the disastrous Mier expedition. Afterwards he served in the Confederate Army, and is depicted here wearing the distinctive uniform of the Kentucky State Guard.

redundant) soldiers, and three "commissioners" who were also tasked with organizing annexation. Unfortunately, while the Santa Fe authorities had no love for the distant central government in Mexico City, they positively hated the Texians. Consequently the expedition finally arrived at Santa Fe, exhausted and hungry, only to find Mexican *Defensores* or local militia and *Presidiales* waiting for them. After one of the Texian officers, Lieutenant William Lewis of the artillery, treacherously persuaded the advance guard to lay down its arms on 17 September, the main body also surrendered without a fight at Laguna Colorado on 5 October. Texas was left without an army.

1841–42: the return of Houston and Santa Anna

On 13 December 1841, Sam Houston resumed office as president, with the firm intention of reversing Lamar's expansionist policies – although he was too late to prevent the departure of the navy, which had just been hired by the rebel state of Yucatan. Since San Jacinto the Mexican government had been preoccupied by political crises, domestic insurrections and the so-called "Pastry War" with France; but the Santa Fe débâcle coincided with the return to power of General Santa Anna, who resumed overt hostilities with Texas. On 5 March 1842 a small Mexican army led by General Rafael Vasquez occupied San Antonio, causing panic among the border

This useful illustration of Texian militia appeared in the *Illustrated London News* in 1842. Note that two of the four figures are either *Tejanos* or Native Americans.

settlements before it pulled out again two days later. In response, large numbers of Texian volunteers rushed to San Antonio, and Houston hastily ordered General Alexander Somervell to go there and take command of them. However, by the time he arrived the volunteers had already elected Edward Burleson to lead them, and in the confusion Vasquez got clean away.

Throughout the summer of 1842 pressure mounted in Texas for an all-out war with Mexico, and in late June there was another clash on the Nueces between Antonio Canales (now a *Centralista* brigadier-general) and a battalion of Texian and US-raised volunteers under General James Davis. Despite this, President Houston still held back; from the very beginning of the Revolution he had been committed to the annexation of Texas by the United States, and he had no wish then or at any other time to become embroiled in Mexican adventures. Unfortunately, just as it was beginning to seem that he would be successful in delaying any action until the onset of bad weather made it impossible, the Mexicans struck again.

On 11 September another Mexican army, led this time by General Woll, attacked San Antonio and captured Chauncey Johnson's militia company after a six-hour battle. Unlike Vasquez, General Woll then sat tight, and was still occupying the town when a combined force of Rangers and Volunteers led by Jack Hays and "Old Paint" Caldwell turned up on 17 September. At first the resulting battle of Salado Creek looked like a re-run of the Concepcion fight in 1835, as dug-in Texian riflemen inflicted heavy casualties on Woll's regulars. However, the course of events changed when Captain Nicholas Dawson and his Fayette County militia company were caught in the open as they marched towards the sound of the guns. Despite taking refuge in a mesquite grove they were thoroughly worked over by Woll's artillery, and the survivors were taken prisoner. As a result Woll was able to make an almost unimpeded withdrawal two days later, and Houston then had no alternative but to authorize a retaliatory strike after all.

1842–43: the Laredo and Santa Fe expeditions

Command of the expeditions was again given to Alexander Somervell, who was widely regarded as weak, indecisive, and quite incapable of inspiring any confidence in his men. On the other hand, he could be trusted to follow orders: President Houston wanted a demonstration, not a dashing raid deep into Mexico. True to form, Somervell did not actually set off from San Antonio until 25 November 1842, and even then – despite being mounted – his 750 men took two weeks to reach Laredo, which was then still a Mexican town. Cold, wet, short of food and other supplies, the unruly volunteers plundered the town, and then moved

Colonel Ed Burleson (1798–1851). Born in North Carolina, Burleson first served under his father in the War of 1812 before moving to Texas in 1830. With a solid reputation as an Indian fighter, he was elected commander of the Army of the People in succession to Stephen Austin. He commanded the 1st Texas Regiment at San Jacinto, and served the Republic variously as major-general of militia, colonel of the Frontier Regiment, and vice-president to Sam Houston. (Texas State Library and Archives ommission)

After being taken prisoner in the Mier débâcle, Captain Ewen Cameron was singled out for execution, probably because he and his "rangers" had been making a thorough nuisance of themselves in the Nueces Strip for years. Note that he appears to be wearing frontier clothing with a dragoon's shoulder scales as a badge of rank.

off down the Rio Grande valley to Guerrero. After three days 187 of the men turned for home in disgust; and on 19 December Somervell himself ordered an end to the expeditions

However, a number of volunteers refused to follow him and, electing William Fisher to command them, they crossed the Rio Grande and attacked the town of Mier on 26 December. This turned out to be a mistake, for it was heavily defended by both Mexican regulars under General Ampudia, and *Defensores* under Canales. Outnumbered two to one, the Texians again inflicted heavy casualties on the Mexicans; but they proved too undisciplined to exploit their initial success, and were eventually surrounded and compelled to surrender. The prisoners were marched into the interior, and a number of them – selected by lot – were shot after an unsuccessful escape attempt near Saltillo; the rest were held captive until November 1844. In military terms the affair was a minor one, and perhaps the most significant feature of it was Ampudia's willingness to treat his captives as prisoners of war rather than executing them out of hand as rebels. However, this débâcle, coming so soon after the loss of the regulars at Santa Fe, also provided a salutory shock to Texian confidence.

Even more ignominious in its way was the final campaign. In spring 1843 an independent partisan corps, rather incongruously calling itself the "Battalion of Invincibles," was led by the former quartermaster general Jacob Snively on another raid to Santa Fe. This time they had the openly piratical purpose of attacking Mexican wagon trains; instead, they encountered – and defeated – Mexican troops, only to be arrested at the end of June by US dragoons sent to the area to protect the Mexican wagon trains. Despite this embarrassing episode, negotiations to join the Union proceeded apace; and in July 1845, within a few short months of the return of the prisoners taken at Mier, US regulars were encamped along the Nueces in preparation for annexation and the inevitable war with Mexico.[4]

ORGANIZATION: THE REVOLUTION

There was no formal militia organization in Texas prior to the Revolution, and the initial fighting on the outbreak of the revolt was undertaken by spontaneously raised local volunteer companies. Actuated by a very conscious and deep-seated American "minute man" tradition of turning out in times of danger to the community, they elected their own officers, largely decided their actions by consensus, and then (just as spontaneously) returned home again just as soon as their individual domestic concerns outweighed public ones.

These were the men who, calling themselves the "Army of the People," fought well at Gonzales and Concepcion; but when set to the tedium of blockading Bexar they soon began drifting away, particularly as the weather grew colder and the planting season approached. From a probable high of nearly 900 men they were reduced to about one-third of that number when Ben Milam finally stormed the town in early December. Even then the overwhelming majority of those who actually took part in the assault were not Texians at all but recently arrived volunteers from the United States.

4 See Essential Histories 25, *The Mexican War 1846–48*

The Regular Army of Texas

In the meantime, at the urging of Sam Houston, who had long ago served under the legendary Andrew Jackson, the Texian provisional government rather prematurely resolved on 13 November 1835 to establish a regular force of 1,120 men under his command. Then, realizing they were probably putting the cart before the horse, they also instructed a military committee to decide how these men should be organized. A week later the committee duly reported back that:

"If the belligerent state of Texas did not warrant, and the Convention had not decreed, that a part of the active force should consist of Permanent Volunteers from the United States, and elsewhere, your committee would not have been at a loss for a moment to determine and classify the regular army of Texas; but, inasmuch as we shall receive a large body of volunteers from the United States, who must place themselves in the list of that class, and the majority of whom will be riflemen.

"Your committee have deemed it more conducive to the perfect organisation of the army, to constitute one entire regiment of Artillery, and one entire regiment of Infantry. This classification is predicated upon the fact that the immediate defence of the sea coast, agreeably to the resolution and decree of the Convention, will require five companies of artillery at the various points therein indicated, and that there will be required for offensive operations in the ensuing campaign against San Antonio de Bexar, one battalion, or five companies more.

"Your committee would therefore recommend the following organisation of the regular army, viz:

One regiment of Artillery   560 men
One regiment of Infantry   560 men
Total number of rank and file,
  as per decree   1120

"In this organisation it follows that each regiment will consist of two battalions, each battalion of five companies, and each company of fifty-six rank and file."

A lieutenant-colonel was supposed to command one infantry battalion and a major the other. Each company was to be commanded by a captain, assisted by a lieutenant, a second lieutenant, four sergeants and four corporals, all ranked in order of precedence. The artillery establishment was similar but included an additional major, and a third lieutenant in each company.

This report, embodied as an "Act to raise a regular army" and passed on 24 November, was to be the guiding principle behind all of the regular forces in the service of what became the Republic of Texas. While most other countries relied first and foremost upon a professional standing army, supported as and when necessary by militia and other more or less irregular volunteers, the Texians took the opposite view. As the committee's recommendation makes clear, it was envisaged that the greater number of the soldiers would be untrained (and undisciplined) militia and volunteers largely armed with rifles. Therefore it was the

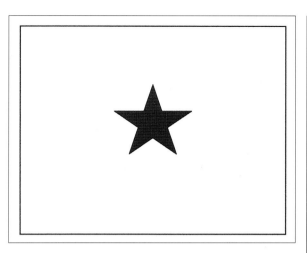

An early version of the Lone Star flag – dark blue on white – which may have been carried at San Jacinto in 1836. MacLaughlin's sketches of the Mier expedition also depict a similar flag, though in that case it is unclear whether the star was blue or red.

regular army that was to serve in a supporting role – hence what at first sight appears to be an unusually high proportion of artillerymen.

The theory had much to commend it, but the problem both during the Revolution and afterwards was finding enough men willing to enlist as regular soldiers. Even the United States Army had trouble in finding recruits in this era, and substantially filled its ranks with newly arrived immigrants and the ever-present urban poor. However, the great majority of those coming to Texas were sufficiently self-reliant to regard regular soldiering as beneath them; at the very outset the men sitting outside Bexar flatly refused to join the new army, or even to acknowledge Sam Houston's unelected authority. There was indeed a widespread and profound egalitarian prejudice against subjection to military discipline and, as was noted by one commentator on the volunteers serving in the later American Civil War, this Jacksonian spirit of self-reliance meant that "the soldier detested taking orders and the officer shrank from commanding. The soldier would comply with a reasonable order but he did so because it was reasonable, not because it was an order."

Major Robert Morris, one of the New Orleans Grays, rather more trenchantly declared in a letter to Houston that "there are now [29 November 1835] here 225 men, nearly all from the U.S. who on no consideration will enter into any service connected with the Regular Army, the name of which is a perfect Bugbear to them."

Indeed, while the appointment of officers to the regular army was a welcome source of patronage to Texian politicians – even Houston's sole qualification for his appointment as commander-in-chief was the fact that he was a close political crony of the provisional governor, Henry Smith – it was all but impossible to recruit the required rank and file. It has been estimated that no more than 100 men in total ever signed up as regulars during the Revolution. In fact the first body of regular infantry enlisted was an unemployed gang of mercenaries who had originally been recruited in New Orleans for General Mexia's ill-fated expedition to Tampico, and were thus providentially available for hire. Unfortunately, having survived that particular fiasco almost all of them were subsequently killed in the massacre of Fannin's command at Goliad; significantly, at that

Matamoros: this rich port city near the mouth of the Rio Grande played a pivotal role in military operations during the Revolution and afterwards, although it would not be captured until American troops took it in 1846.

time their commander, Captain John Allen, was back in New Orleans looking for new recruits. Throughout the Republic's brief existence the majority of Texian regulars would be mercenaries and filibusters picked up in the Crescent City's saloons and along its cosmopolitan waterfront.

Initially the artillery service was marginally more attractive to Texians, since the technical expertise it demanded made it more "respectable," but most of the original enlistees were killed during the Revolution and few were recruited afterwards. Similarly, although there was apparently no difficulty in finding sufficient one-year enlistees for a battalion of Rangers authorized on 24 November 1835, recruits were even hard to find for the regular cavalry. William Barrett Travis successfully persuaded the government to sanction the raising of a 384-strong regiment under his command, but only 20 men had been signed up by the time he led them to the Alamo.

At San Jacinto, the climactic battle of the Revolution, the 1st Regiment Regular Infantry comprised just a single battalion of four companies, commanded by Lieutenant-Colonel Henry Millard and acting Major John M.Allen, late of the Tampico Blues. The battalion is sometimes described as being composed of US Army deserters, but only two of its own companies were present under Captains Briscoe and Turner, and two others had to be borrowed from the 1st Texas Volunteers. Even then the battalion could only muster a total of just 139 rank and file besides officers and NCOs.

Unfortunately the regular army never recovered from its shaky start (and subsequent battering) during the Revolution. Instead of two

Juan Seguin (1806–90). The most prominent of the *Tejano* supporters of the Revolution, Seguin took part in the defense of the Alamo and led a company at San Jacinto. On 4 June 1836 he accepted the surrender of the Mexican garrison of Bexar, and afterwards held the post with his own 2nd Cavalry. This painting by Jefferson Wright presumably depicts him in the uniform of his regiment – the arrangement of the buttons is certainly consistent with the 1839 regulations, and there appears to be a star on his epaulettes; on the other hand there is no precedent or authority for the very broad gold braid. Having fled to Mexico in 1842, Seguin served for some time with the Mexican army, but was allowed to return to Texas in 1848; he finally retired again to Mexico in 1867. (Texas State Library and Archives Commission)

Federalist flag as authorized by the Texian provisional council, based on the Mexican green/white/red tricolor with black lettering. Notwithstanding popular legend (and numerous films) there is no evidence that this flag was flown over the Alamo, whose defenders favored independence. However, it was certainly carried by James Grant's Federal Volunteer Army when they marched from Bexar at the end of December 1835, and was presumably the one captured by General Urrea's forces at San Patricio.

battalions totalling ten companies as authorized in November 1835, the Republic's 1st Infantry still comprised only a single battalion of four companies by 1838. The 1st Artillery was in an even more parlous state: deficient in both men and guns, the remaining personnel were little more than military storekeepers in charge of munitions. As for the cavalry, judging by the enlistment dates on surviving muster rolls the two companies of Major James Tinsley's 1st Dragoons were founded on that part of the original Cavalry Corps which did not perish with Travis at the Alamo, while the three companies of Lieutenant-Colonel Juan Seguin's 2nd Cavalry were only enlisted for six months from October 1836.

The short enlistment period for the 2nd Cavalry – more consistent with volunteers – was in marked contrast to all the other regulars, who were serving on two-year enlistments that all ran out in the summer of 1838. The four infantry companies were immediately re-mustered for a further three years from 22 August 1838, as apparently were the two companies of the 1st Dragoons which then became the 1st Cavalry under Colonel Lysander Wells.

Shortly after Mirabeau B. Lamar took over as president in December 1838 he accepted Albert Sidney Johnston's recommendation to authorize the consolidation and expansion of all the regulars into a new 15-company-strong "Frontier Regiment" with a theoretical establishment of 840 men. The nucleus of this "new" regiment was Companies A–D of the existing 1st Infantry Regiment, while the 1st Cavalry apparently became Companies E and F. The new regiment

TEXAS!!

Emigrants who are desirious of assisting Texas at this important crisis of her affairs may have a free passage and equipments, by applying at the
NEW-YORK and PHILADELPHIA HOTEL,
On the Old Levee, near the Blue Stores.

Now is the time to ensure a fortune in Land: To all who remain in Texas during the War will be allowed 1280 Acres.
To all who remain Six Months, 640 Acres.
To all who remain Three Months, 320 Acres.
And as Colonists, 4600 Acres for a family and 1470 Acres for a Single Man.
New Orleans, April 23d, 1836.

To avoid legal difficulties this New Orleans recruiting poster coyly solicited "emigrants" rather than soldiers.

OPPOSITE Although this engraving actually depicts Walker's filibusters in Nicaragua in the 1850s, Bexar must have presented a very similar picture as James Grant assembled his Federal Volunteer Army in December 1835.

also absorbed an ordnance detachment under Colonel George Hockley based in the arsenal at Austin; a payroll detachment; and a detachment of "spies" (scouts) under Captain John Lynch. In fact only three new companies were ever completed and no more than 674 men in total were ever carried on the rolls. What was more, the fact that most of the original personnel came from the old 1st Infantry meant that the regiment was almost invariably referred to by that title in official documents – no doubt to the disgust of the cavalry troopers and the other specialists.

Command of the "new" regiment, which thus encompassed the whole of the regular army, went first to Edward Burleson, as colonel, and then to William Gordon Cooke (once of the New Orleans Grays), although Colonel Lysander Wells remained in very independent charge of the two cavalry companies until his untimely death in a duel in May 1840.

The Texian Republic's regular army did not long survive him. In the following March President Lamar was compelled to recognize that for shortage of money it would have to be disbanded, although most of it remained in being long enough to serve in the disastrous Santa Fe expedition. As for the rest, on 10 December 1841 Congress passed a "Joint Resolution for the relief of soldiers composing the late 1st Regiment of Infantry."

The Volunteers
Given the relative insignificance of the regular army and the unreliability of the militia, it is not surprising that the largely American volunteers should have done most of the fighting. From the very beginning of the uprising the Texians were joined by a steady stream of adventurers from the United States, since, as Captain Creed Taylor recalled:

"The filibustering spirit was rife in America during the first half of the nineteenth century, and many adventurers and soldiers of fortune stalked across the pages of history. It was the era of frontier expansion in the United States; and it was a period of unstable conditions in Mexico – the two republics were neighbors, and the great Southwest was the breeding-ground and clearing-house of unrest. The scene of action shifted to Texas during the revolution. The Texan revolt and declaration

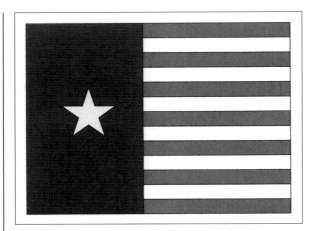

This curious cross between the Lone Star flag and the stars and stripes appears in a contemporary lithograph by A.E.Baker depicting Fannin's 1st Texas Volunteers at Goliad.

Captain Ward's Georgia Battalion carried this white flag with a single blue star and lettering at Goliad; the reverse apparently carried the words *Ubi libertas habitat ibi nostra patria est* ("Where liberty dwells there is my home").

LIBERTY OR DEATH

of war for independence attracted much attention and brought many brave and adventurous young spirits to the scene of action from every part of the American Union and especially from the bordering southwestern states – men of physical courage, daredevils of restless spirit, ever ready and always anxious to hazard their lives in any enterprise or expedition that offered excitement and adventure; and, perchance, gain of treasure as well as added laurels of valor."

The status of these early volunteers was decidedly uncertain, in that while they too had been raised more or less spontaneously in the United States to go and assist the Texians in their struggle, they were not officially in the service of the provisional government. This was pointedly underlined after the fall of Bexar by the readiness with which most of them joined Dr James Grant's filibustering expedition into Mexico, rather than swear allegiance to the Texian government, far less join its embryonic regular army.

Nor were matters much improved by the Council's decision to create two different classes of volunteers. Both were sworn into the service of Texas for six months or the duration of the war, and when discharged the *Permanent Volunteers*, whose officers were appointed by Sam Houston and the Council, were entitled to receive a headright grant of 640 acres of land. The *Auxillary Volunteers* on the other hand were only entitled to 320 acres, but they could and did elect their own officers. Unsurprisingly, the auxiliary service proved more congenial to the individuals, such as David Crockett, making their way from the United States, until Sam Houston's reorganisation of the army during the "Runaway Scrape" effectively abolished the distinction.

While largely conforming to the organizational matrix laid down by the Council – which in any case followed familiar US models – the various volunteer units continued to elect their own officers all the way up to their commander-in-chief as a matter of course, without any reference to the politicians at San Felipe or to anyone else. Those individuals who disagreed with the collective decision, or fell out with their commanding officer – or anybody else, for that matter – still felt themselves perfectly free to transfer to other units more to their liking, or to return home to the United States.

Federal Volunteer Army

This process is clearly illustrated by what happened after the fall of Bexar. Once General Cos had been sent on his way the "Army of the People" simply fell apart. Nearly all of the few remaining Texian militia disbanded and returned home for the planting season, but at the same time fresh companies of eager US volunteers were still turning up in Texas. By mid-December it was estimated that there were some 160 volunteers hanging around at Velasco; 75 at Washington on the Brazos; another 75 at Goliad, and about 300 at Bexar. There Frank Johnson and James Grant set about organizing the grandly titled Federal Volunteer Army in preparation for the proposed expedition to Matamoros. By 17 December they were ready but, well aware of the General Council's sensitivity over the security of Bexar, Johnson reassuringly declared that no move would be made until an adequate garrison had been provided for the post. Notwithstanding, as soon as Johnson's back was turned, Grant decamped with all the horses and every man who could be persuaded to follow him. This left just 104 men at the Alamo under Lieutenant-Colonel James Neill, and to make matters worse another 20 or so were soon marched off to Copano by Captain John Chenoweth.

The remaining garrison then comprised three companies: Captain William Carey's regular artillery, Robert White's Bexar Guards, and William Blazeby's New Orleans Grays. The other company of New Orleans Grays, now calling itself the San Antonio Grays, had elected to go off with Grant – as did about 20 or 30 of Blazeby's men, who transferred to Captain Burke's Mobile Grays. Conversely, a number of Cooke's San Antonio Grays were left behind at Bexar: some from choice, others because they lacked horses, but for the most part because they were lying sick or wounded in the hospital. At Goliad, Sam Houston persuaded about 20 men to enlist under Captain William Baker and return with James Bowie to Bexar, to replace the men taken by Chenoweth. Eventually the Alamo garrison would also be joined by ten men under a Captain William Patton; 12 Tennessee Mounted Rifles led by Captain William Harrison; 20 regular cavalry under Lieutenant-Colonel William Travis; and ultimately by 30-odd men of the Gonzales Ranging Company.

In the meantime, when it left Goliad, Colonel James Grant's Federal Volunteer Army comprised a single battalion of some 209 men organized in six companies commanded by Captains William Cooke, David Burke, H.R.A.Wigginton, B.L.Lawrence, Thomas Pearson and Thomas Llewellyn.

Unfortunately for Grant, further down the road at Refugio, Houston – who had been employing his talents for character assassination to the full – made another very spirited appeal to the volunteers which, as William Cooke rather dramatically reported, "completely defeated the object of Col Grant." The actual result was that both the San Antonio Grays and Mobile Grays (now commanded by Samuel Pettus) agreed to enlist as auxiliary volunteers, and to wait at Refugio for the arrival of Colonel Fannin; while Wigginton's and Lawrence's companies broke up, many of the soldiers returning to the United States. At first sight it would appear that only Pearson's and Llewellyn's companies stuck by Grant, but on closer examination a rather more complex picture emerges. Some men from those companies also opted to stay at Refugio, while a number of individuals from other units took their place, and

Captain William Scott's Lynchburg Volunteers carried this blue flag with a white star and lettering at Bexar, and afterwards with Dimmitt at Goliad. It may possibly have been this, rather than Dimmitt's rather better known "bloody arm" flag, which led to the confrontation with Grant's Federal Volunteers, since Reuben Brown referred to Dimmitt raising "the flag of independence".

this process continued for some time afterwards. Pearson's company were nominally artillery, possessing three brass cannon, and when Fannin appropriated the guns in mid-February some of the gunners went with them; they were apparently replaced by a similar number of former New Orleans Grays from Cooke's and Pettus' companies.

Not all of these transfers were voluntary. Sometimes, as at Bexar, they were the result of men being left behind in hospitals, or simply through random circumstances. It is certainly significant that since Captain Pearson's men were initially left with the guns at San Patricio, Llewellyn's company had the pick of the horses run off during Grant's early raids into the Rio Grande country. Then, when the whole force split up at Santa Rosa on 23 February, Grant kept all the best mounted men with himself and let Johnson (who had finally caught up) take the others back to San Patricio. Consequently, when Johnson was defeated there on 27 February, the majority of his men naturally belonged to Pearson's ill-mounted company, although there was also a platoon of Llewellyn's men under Sergeant Pittman. Conversely, Grant's party which was wiped out at Agua Dulce four days later was mainly comprised of Llewellyn's men, but did include a few of Pearson's who had found themselves decent horses.

Texas Volunteers

Meanwhile the main body of the volunteers back at Refugio, now under the rather uncertain command of Colonel James Walker Fannin, comprised Ward's "Georgia Battalion," together with those elements of Grant's command which had elected to take the oath as auxiliary volunteers, and a number of other independent volunteer and regular

In addition to the Mexican Army, the Texians also had to contend with the ever-present threat posed by the Comanches.

units. There it soon began to dawn on Fannin that since his notional commander-in-chief, Sam Houston, had given up on finding anybody willing to take orders from him and had gone off on indefinite leave, he, Fannin, was probably now in overall command of the Texian army.

Unsettled by this notion, he fell back to Goliad on 12 February and there reorganized his disparate forces into the "1st Provisional Regiment of Texas Volunteers." Despite his intense and strongly expressed dislike of elections, Fannin gritted his teeth for long enough to have himself voted as its colonel, and William Ward of the Georgia Battalion as its lieutenant-colonel. The regiment, then numbering about 300 men, comprised two infantry battalions broadly organized on the lines earlier set out by the government.

The first or Georgia Battalion, which had actually been organized by Ward back at Velasco, comprised three companies from Georgia under William Wadsworth, Uriah Bullock and James Winn, and Isaac Ticknor's Alabama Grays. After the elections the battalion was commanded by Major Warren C.Mitchell. The second or Lafayette Battalion, organized

The attempted breakout at Saltillo of the Texian prisoners from Fisher's failed attempt on the town of Mier; sketch by Charles McLaughlin, one of the volunteers who took part in the Mier expedition.

The "Black Bean" episode, as depicted by McLaughlin with a wealth of clothing detail. After their unsuccessful attempt to escape the Texians were compelled to draw lots, using beans, before being decimated by firing squad.

at Goliad under the command of Major Benjamin C.Wallace, was of rather more mixed origin: the San Antonio Grays and Mobile Grays came from Grant's "army", while Captain Benjamin Bradford's Huntsville Volunteers had previously been occupying Goliad, and Burr Duval's and Jack Shackleford's companies were recent arrivals from the United States. Also under Fannin's command but not absorbed into the 1st Texas Volunteers were a number of smaller units, including Captain Amon B.King's Paducah Volunteers, and Captain Albert C.Horton's locally recruited Matagorda Volunteers. Horton and a number of his men were mounted and provided Fannin with his only cavalry.

There were even two companies of regulars. The first, led by Captain Ira Westover, was a composite unit formed from Allen's Tampico Blues and his own artillerymen. The second was a Mexican regular artillery company commanded by Captain Luis Guerra; the captain and his men were *Federalistas* who had rather unwisely defected to General Mexia's forces during his abortive attack on Tampico, and were then forced to flee back to Texas with him. At first they were happy enough to join with the then pro-Federalist Texian insurgents; but the Texian declaration of independence on 2 March placed them in a difficult position, and Fannin was obliged to grant them an honorable discharge on 11 March. In their place he raised a new artillery company commanded by Captain Stephen Durst, largely around a nucleus of gunners from Pearson's company who had come back from San Patricio.

Of the various other units somewhere in the vicinity but not under Fannin's control, the largest was Colonel Edwin Morehouse's

(continued on page 33)

THE ARMY OF THE PEOPLE, 1835
1: Texian militiaman
2: *Tejano* scout
3: Texian militiaman

A

VOLUNTEERS, 1836
1: Dr James Grant
2: Volunteer, Capt Shackleford's "Red Rovers"
3: Volunteer, New Orleans Grays

B

REGULARS AT SAN JACINTO, 1836
1: Private, 1st Regt of Infantry
2: Major John Allen, 1st Infantry
3: Deserter, US 7th Infantry

C

REGULAR INFANTRY, 1836–41
1: Private, 1st Regt of Infantry, 1836
2: Private, 1st Regt of Infantry, 1840
3: First Sergeant in full dress

D

REGULAR OFFICERS, 1839–41
1: Colonel William Gordon Cooke
2: Ordnance officer
3: Captain of Infantry

E

THE CAVALRY
1: Colonel Lysander Wells, 1840
2: Trooper in service dress, 1840
3: Officer in service dress

F

VOLUNTEERS, 1842
1: Trooper, Galveston Hussars
2: Galveston Coast Guard
3: Texas Ranger

G

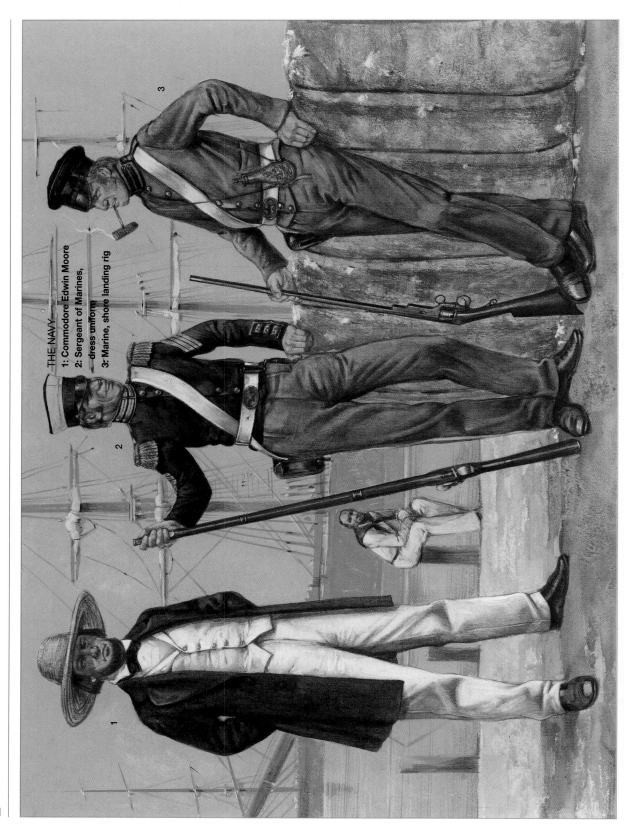

THE NAVY
1: Commodore Edwin Moore
2: Sergeant of Marines,
   dress uniform
3: Marine, shore landing rig

190-strong New York Battalion. Sadly, they were delayed by a series of accidents en route to Texas – which included being detained for a time in Bermuda on suspicion of piracy; neither they, nor Chenoweth's men at Copano, nor any other intended reinforcements ever did succeed in joining Fannin.

With the exception of those anticipated reinforcements, both Grant's and Fannin's entire commands were effectively wiped out by General Urrea's forces in a brisk series of actions between 27 February and 19 March 1836. Most of the survivors were subsequently executed at Goliad on 27 March, and comparatively few of them survived either as prisoners or as fugitives. Together with the loss of the volunteers at the Alamo on 6 March, this meant that the Texian army more or less had to be reconstructed from scratch.

San Jacinto

This battle was the otherwise overrated Sam Houston's real achievement. In the face of the Mexican advance both Travis and Fannin had desperately appealed for support from the Texian militia; but apart from Hugh Fraser's Refugio militia, who had provided Fannin with guides and couriers, and the Gonzales men who famously slipped into the Alamo during the siege, no help actually materialized.

On 4 March, Houston contrived to have himself reappointed as commander-in-chief, and this time with authority over all the Texian forces and not just the regulars. However, it was not until a week later that he arrived at Gonzales to take command of the 374-strong Alamo relief force. Two days later the news that the mission had already fallen sent him back in headlong retreat to the Colorado river. Enough Texian militia joined him at Beason's Crossing to raise his total strength to 1,400 men, before the news of Fannin's surrender sent him tumbling back again. By the time he eventually halted at Groce's Plantation on the Brazos he was again down to some 500 men, but the retreat at least ensured that the Texian forces had broken contact. Houston was thus able to spend the next two weeks pulling the army together and putting it into a fit state to fight a proper battle.

The composition of that army, which won the last-gasp victory at San Jacinto on 21 April, is fairly well documented. Aside from a number of detachments that were absent for a variety of reasons, the infantry were organized in three regiments – or rather, into one battalion of "regulars" and two regiments of "volunteers'.

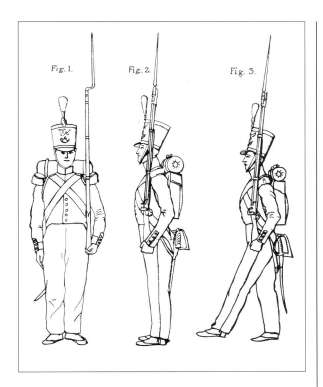

US regulars in dress uniforms, as depicted in Winfield Scott's *Tactics*. This drill book was employed by the Texian Army; but while A.S.Johnston aspired to give them similar uniforms, it appears that he never did manage to provide shakos.

Another variant of the lone-star-and-stripes flag, sometimes known as the "Hawkins Flag". This was adopted during the Revolution and afterwards used by the Texas Navy.

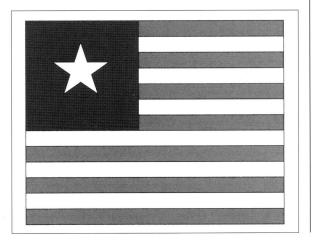

Samuel Walker (1817–47). Depicted here in US uniform, he came to Texas in 1842 and was taken prisoner during the Mier expedition. Afterwards he served in the Texas Rangers under Jack Hays; collaborated with Samuel Colt in designing an improved revolver; and was killed in Mexico during the war of 1846–48.

The 1st Texas Volunteers (not to be confused with Fannin's similarly titled regiment) was commanded by Colonel Edward Burleson and Lieutenant-Colonel Alexander Somervell. It was in fact largely made up of Texian militiamen. It not only lent two companies to the 1st Regulars, but Kuykendall's Company E was guarding the baggage and sick, and for some reason it had no Company G. It therefore took the field at San Jacinto with only six companies, mustering a total of 257 rank and file.

The 2nd Texas Volunteers, commanded by Colonel Sidney Sherman and Lieutenant-Colonel Joseph Bennett, had ten infantry companies at San Jacinto, but they were a rather more *ad hoc* grouping hastily formed at Groce's Plantation around a cadre from the 1st Texas, and comprised both Texian militia and US volunteer companies. For some reason quite a high proportion of the men were absent sick or guarding the baggage, and it therefore totalled only 269 rank and file present for duty on 21 April.

The artillery had just 20 men and two guns under the command of Lieutenant-Colonel James Neill and Captain Isaac Moreland; while the cavalry, attached for administrative purposes to the 2nd Texas Volunteers, comprised two troops numbering a total of 51 men under the overall command of Mirabeau B.Lamar (who held no official rank) and Captain Henry Karnes.

In spite of Houston's reluctance to fight, his men won a resounding victory at San Jacinto at a cost of just nine killed and 30 wounded; but afterwards most of them promptly went home, requiring the army to be almost completely reconstituted all over again.

THE ARMY OF THE REPUBLIC

Ironically, the army of Texas attained its greatest strength after the war was over. In addition to the patchwork of militia, regulars, permanent volunteers and auxiliary volunteers who had done all the fighting, the General Council also authorized the raising of a Reserve Army, which was to be organized, clothed and equipped in the United States before entering Texas as a complete body. Once these various elements were more or less consolidated, the army was some 2,000 strong by December 1836.

The new generation of volunteers were still rather loosely organized and, as during the Revolution, rather too many of them continued to operate independently, which hardly helped the serious disciplinary problems. The major part of the army comprised two infantry "brigades" each of two regiments. On 20 December 1836 each of the four regiments was authorized to have ten companies, but surviving muster rolls indicate that they may not have attained this strength.

Initially the first volunteer brigade was commanded by Edwin Morehouse and built around a nucleus of his own New Yorkers and Charles Harrison's large Kentucky battalion. The second brigade, originally the Reserve Army, commanded by Thomas Jefferson Green, comprised Green's own and Colonel J.H.Milroy's battalions. By the end of the year both brigadiers had been replaced by Thomas Jefferson Rusk and Felix Huston respectively, while Sam Houston was still nominally major-general. In practice, since he was fully occupied with his political duties, the army was actually commanded by the senior brigadier – which is what led to the duel between Felix Huston and A.S.Johnston.

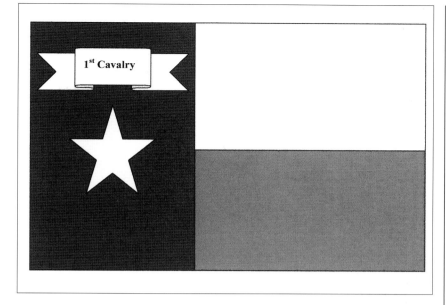

Regimental standard of the 1st Cavalry, in blue, white and red with white charges and black lettering, as prescribed in the 1839 regulations. Essentially it is the flag of the Republic (and the state) of Texas.

Militia

Having furloughed or disbanded all or most of the unruly volunteers in the summer of 1837, Houston proposed instead to defend Texas with a reorganized militia. In the previous December the Texian Congress had passed legislation which ought to have established two divisions, each commanded by a major-general and each comprising two brigades of two regiments. Unfortunately the Congress declined to appropriate the necessary funds to support this organization, and it was not until after the demise of the volunteer army that the militia was finally set on a proper footing; by then the four brigades were organized in just a single division.

Thomas J.Rusk held the major-general's position in command of the militia for most of the period, with the exception of four years 1839–43 when Felix Huston contrived to get the job, and after 1844 when Sidney Sherman took over. In practice, of course, this was only an administrative organization, and militia companies were mobilized individually as and when required. In contrast to the *ad hoc* companies which had formed more or less spontaneously during the Revolution, this new militia was supposed to be raised by conscription. Additionally, in the best American military tradition, there were a growing number of volunteer militia units bearing such titles as the Milam Guards and the Travis Guards. As a result, the Texian forces commanded by the ever-pugnacious Ed Burleson at Plum Creek were

Company guidon, in white on blue, as prescribed for cavalry in the 1839 regulations; the company letter was to be placed in the center of the star.

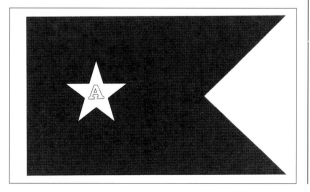

Hall's breech-loading carbine was standard issue to US Army Dragoons and may also have been used by the Texians pending the arrival of the Jenks carbine.

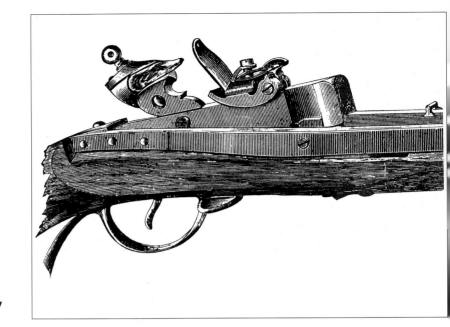

Samuel Colt's revolving pistols and carbines were first used in Texas, and although popularly associated with the Texas Rangers were also employed by the regular army and the navy.

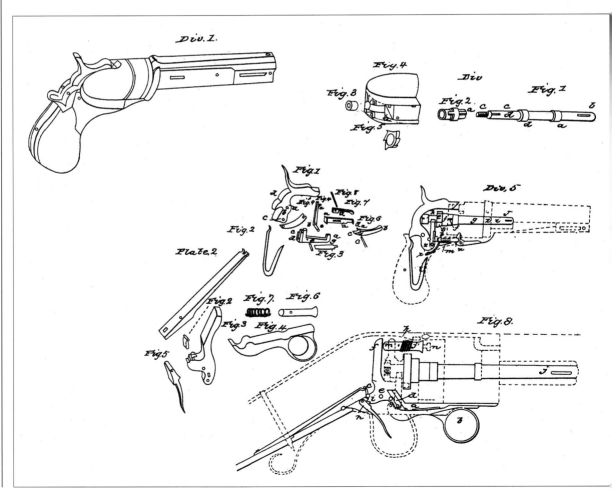

John Coffee Hays (1817–83). Born in Tennessee, "Jack" Hays came to Texas in 1836, just in time to help bury the victims of the Goliad massacre. He made his name as an officer of the Texas Rangers; credited with introducing the Colt's revolver, he served with some distinction during the US-Mexican War and afterwards moved on to California.

substantially made up of what can most charitably be described as irregulars. Bowing to the inevitable, the Congress eventually authorized 20 frontier counties to organize "minutemen companies" under the jurisdiction of the county judges. This was in effect a return to the old volunteer militias of the Revolution.

And then, of course, there were the famous Texas Rangers. In addition to a properly enlisted battalion-sized unit under Colonel Robert Coleman, there were a considerable number of semi-piratical independent companies variously and quite promiscuously designated as "rangers", "mounted gunmen", "mounted volunteers", "mounted riflemen" and "spies." As the last indicates, these early Texas Rangers were not combat units *per se*, but primarily tasked with scouting and

**Ben McCulloch (1811–62).
Born in Tennessee, he fought
as an artilleryman at San
Jacinto; became a noted
Ranger officer; and as a
Confederate general was killed
at Pea Ridge, Arkansas, in 1862.**

reconnaissance – although it was not unknown for some of them to become involved in extra-curricular activities such as cattle-rustling, particularly in the disputed Nueces Strip.

Although the militia companies, acting in conjunction with the Rangers, proved at least reasonably effective in combating the ever-present Comanche threat, they were less than capable of dealing with the large-scale Mexican incursions which commenced in 1842.

South Western Army of Operations

A number of volunteer companies had to be enlisted for three months' service from 10 or 11 March 1842. Only ten of the companies were actually committed to the ineffectual operations against Vasquez, while most of the others – including Captain John Howe's Galveston Artillery, which had actually been authorized by Congress as long ago as 30 January 1841 – were chiefly employed in defending key locations such as Galveston itself. A couple of units, the Galveston Coast Guards and the Galveston Fusiliers, were even embarked on the steamer *Lafitte* and set to patrolling for any signs of a Mexican invasion fleet.

In the meantime the inevitable rush of US volunteers began flocking to Texas, where many of them were assembled into a regiment (or rather, a battalion) of seven companies under General James Davis. Another five companies included the Missouri Invincibles and the Union Guards, though it is unclear whether they were part of Davis' largely Texian regiment or whether they formed a separate unit. Both Americans and Texians were involved in the defense of Lipantitlan, near Corpus Christi, against Canales' raid in late June; but their enlistments ran out in October, and therefore none of them crossed the border as part of Somervell's grandly titled "South Western Army of Operations."

Somervell's force which marched on Laredo comprised 18 companies of Texian volunteers and conscripted militia, organized into two provisional battalions under Colonels Joseph Bennett and James Cook, and a company of Rangers under the celebrated Jack Hays. When Somervell ordered the expedition to return to San Antonio, those who elected to follow William Fisher on the unauthorized raid across the Rio Grande formed a new battalion of six companies. Unfortunately Fisher's Battalion was a throwback to the old Army of the People; despite having elected new officers to all but Company A, the men were in no wise disposed to take orders from them, and the disaster which followed was perhaps inevitable. Significantly, however, although Hays and his Rangers agreed to do some scouting for the dissidents, they had more sense than to get embroiled in the débâcle at Mier, and thus survived to form the nucleus of the next generation of Texan volunteers – in the service of the United States.

THE PLATES

A: THE ARMY OF THE PEOPLE, 1835

Long afterwards, Creed Taylor recalled that the Texian militia who fought at Gonzales and marched on Bexar "presented an appearance strangely in contrast with the gaily uniformed 'dude' soldiers one may see on dress parade at fairs and military reviews of the present day. Every man carried a long flintlock, muzzle-loading rifle, with shot pouch and powder horn. Most of the men wore buckskin breeches and hunting shirts or jackets, and these garments, from wear and exposure, presented a variety of colors, from a bright yellow to a glossy black, and as to headgear every style was in evidence, from the coonskin cap to the high-crowned 'sombrero.' Nearly all wore shoes, some moccasins, and these were handmade from home-tanned leather. Boots were then not much in vogue, and I believe I am safe in saying there was not a pair in the army at Gonzales; in fact, the only pair of boots I remember seeing during the campaign were worn by General Houston when he visited the army on the Cibolo. All the men carried large knives in a sheath attached to their belts and some carried pistols of various patterns, fashioned after the ideas of local gunsmiths, of that day. Occasionally one would see a double-barrelled pistol, but these were rare, nearly all being of the single-barrelled type and were either carried at the belt or in a holster at the horn of the saddle."

A1: Texian militiaman

Based on illustrations of Western hunting dress in a sketchbook compiled by Alfred J.Miller in 1837, this volunteer wears the near universal fringed jacket/shirt and buckskin breeches. The hunting shirt was a loosely cut garment, usually made of home-spun linen or linsey-woolsey – the fringing originally served to prevent fraying; but buckskin was becoming popular, especially on the plains, where its windproof qualities were more highly prized than the greater ease of drying out linen ones. Buckskin breeches or trousers were very hard wearing and, as depicted here, were almost invariably seamed on the outside for comfort,

with the excess cut into fringing. Nearly all Texians possessed rifles, both for casual hunting and for protection against marauding Comanches. This one is a pretty typical example made by J.J. Henry. As a matter of course two wooden ramrods were carried to guard against untimely breakages; the rag stuffed in the muzzle serves both as a reminder that one ramrod is being carried inside the barrel, and for wiping it clean. Ammunition is carried in the powder horn and bullet bag, and the ensemble is completed by an all-purpose "butcher" knife in the belt.

A2: *Tejano* scout

The contribution made by the federalist *Tejanos* during the Revolution was largely overlooked afterwards as they became swamped by an ever increasing flood of immigrants from the United States. Yet at the time they provided the insurgents with vital supplies and local knowledge, and also provided a useful conduit of communication with the *Federalistas* of the interior. Unfortunately, the Texian declaration of independence on 2 March 1836 forced them to choose between Mexico and Texas, and while some (including Captain Guerra's artillery company) then made their peace with the *Centralistas*, others served under Juan Seguin in the ranks of the 2nd Texas Volunteers at San Jacinto.

Guerra's artillerymen no doubt wore their Mexican Army uniforms while serving under Fannin, but this rather more typical insurgent wears the characteristic short breeches of the *ranchero*, loose white linen shirt and drawers, and a large

Frontier headgear, after sketches by Alfred J. Miller in 1837. According to Miller's notes, the hoods in the top row were made from old blankets – not from actual animal scalps – and apart from being practical and comfortable they will have served to disguise the very distinctive shape of the human head when stalking. Hats are invariably depicted as battered and usually with small brims. The fairly common style at bottom left may in fact be a knitted cap. While Miller often depicts beards they are never very full and obviously result from neglect of shaving when hunting rather than a conscious decision to cultivate them.

blanket or *poncho*. When mounted, leather leggings – or "chaps" as they became known – were strapped on for protection against the chapparal. He is armed with a Mexican carbine or *escopeta* of a style often carried by *Presidiales*.

A3: Texian militiaman

Again based on Miller's sketches, he wears a hooded woolen blanket coat or *capote* of a style very popular on the frontier. Most of those depicted by Miller appear to be blue in color, but green ones are more commonly described in Texas and along the Red River; the noted Texian scout Erasmus "Deaf" Smith was certainly seen by a member of the New Orleans Grays wearing a green capote at the siege of Bexar in 1835. Instead of buckskin breeches he wears trousers made of "Texas jeans," a homespun butternut-colored wool and linen or cotton mix. This particular individual is armed with a Henry "English Pattern" trade rifle, but there is anecdotal evidence that longer-barreled weapons were preferred by many.

B: VOLUNTEERS, 1836

The volunteers from "the old states" depicted in this plate are very closely based on a number of useful sketches drawn from life in nearby Missouri in the 1840s by the noted genre artist George Caleb Bingham.

B1: Dr James Grant

Born at Milton of Redcastle near Inverness, Scotland, in 1793, Grant was originally a surgeon in the East India Company service, but in 1823 he abandoned his wife and family and moved to Mexico. By 1835 he was secretary of the Coahuila y Tejas legislature, but was forced to flee to Texas, where he proceeded to raise a force for a filibustering attempt to establish a new Republic of Northern Mexico, only to be ambushed by General Urrea at Agua Dulce on 2 March 1836. The engagement was a disaster, since the Americans "were bringing on a large herd of horses, and in the attempt to save them and at the same time fight the enemy, who amounted to 150, they were cut to pieces." Grant, depicted here carrying a fine English-made Mortimer rifle, could have escaped; but instead he sent off a messenger to warn Fannin at Goliad, and then he and his ADC, a Georgian named Reuben Brown, determined "to go in and die with the boys."

The battle was already all but over, and "As Grant and myself approached to join our party, the dragoons opened their line and we passed in. We at once saw that some of our party had already been killed, and we decided to sell our lives as dearly as possible. My horse was quickly killed with a lance, but Grant told me to mount Maj. Morris' horse, as Morris had just been killed. I did so, but without seeing any object to be accomplished by it. Just at that moment the horses took a stampede, and broke the lines of

An 1830s illustration of hunting clothes. An old Texas proverb declared that it was "A great country for men and dogs, but hell on women and horses."

dragoons, and Grant and myself finding ourselves the only survivors of our party, followed in the wake of the horses, the dragoons shooting after us, and wounding our horses in several places, but not badly. As we were flying a dragoon rushed upon me with his lance set, but I knocked it one side and shot him, holding my pistol almost against his breast; and scarcely stopping, I fled with Grant, the Mexicans following, and some of them occasionally coming up with us, and crying out to us to surrender and our lives would be saved. But we knew better, and continued to fly, but the number of those overtaking us became larger and larger, and after we had run six or seven miles, they surrounded us, when, seeing no further chance of escape, we dismounted, determined to make them pay dearly for our lives. As I reached the ground a Mexican lanced me in the arm, but Grant immediately shot him dead, when I seized his lance to defend myself. Just as he shot the Mexican I saw Grant fall, pierced with several lances… After Grant fell I saw some ten or a dozen officers go up and run their sword through his body. He was well known to them, having lived a long time in Mexico. They had a bit of a grudge against him."

B2: Volunteer, Captain Jack Shackleford's "Red Rovers"

Raised by Dr Shackleford in Courtland, Alabama, this company's nickname came from their bright red hunting shirts. According to at least one source, bright red jeancloth trousers were also worn together with fur caps, rather than the brown Texas jeans and

straw hat depicted here. Like most US volunteers they were well equipped; the state of Alabama was paid $600 for 50 muskets and accoutrements, while a further $60 was paid for tents and camp equippage, $30 for a set of "amputating instruments and box medicine", and $12 for a bass drum and a side drum! Colonel Fannin duly certified this particular account for payment, but declined to pass another for $210 incurred by the Georgia Battalion, "being for articles furnished them for private purposes, to wit seventy gallons of Brandy"... . Similarly the Huntsville Volunteers, commanded first by Peyton Wyatt and then by Benjamin Bradford, borrowed "fifty first rate U.S. muskets" from the state of Alabama (presumably 1816 pattern Springfields); while Bullock's and Winn's companies were armed with new US "yagers" or 1817 pattern Common Rifles borrowed from the state of Georgia. The volunteers generally also carried military knapsacks; Abel Morgan, who survived the massacre at Goliad, related that when the Mexican soldiers returned "they laid down the bloody clothes and knapsacks they had taken from the dead men... The knapsack that was in front of me had the name of [Edwin] Wingate on it."

B3: Volunteer, New Orleans Grays
Captain Reuben Potter, who saw two or three of the New Orleans Grays arrive as prisoners in Matamoros, recalled that they wore "plain grey jackets, trousers and forage caps." A soldier in Cooke's company named Ebenezer Heath wrote home to Massachusetts that "the color of our uniform was a grey jacket & pants with a sealskin cap." Similarly a German volunteer in the same company named Herman Ehrenberg recorded that "We all quickly purchased ourselves clothing, grey in colour, fit for life on the prairie, which we found ready-made in the numerous stores, from which the name of our company was derived." Readers misled by a careless translation of Ehrenberg's *Kleider* as "uniforms" rather than simply as "clothing" have contributed to a widespread belief that the two companies of New Orleans Grays were dressed in US Army surplus gray fatigue uniforms; but no contemporary source actually says so.

Instead, contemporary trade advertisements show in New Orleans newspapers show that ready-made clothing, "fit for life on the prairie" was readily available in the city's stores, simply because gray or butternut jeancloth pants and roundabouts were the ordinary workwear of that time in the South. In other words, not only did the New Orleans Grays hurriedly go out and buy themselves the contemporary equivalent of chinos, but other volunteer units such as David Burke's Mobile Grays and Isaac Ticknor's Alabama Grays (and indeed the Texian government's own purchasing agents) were undoubtedly doing exactly the same.

With even less excuse, some modern reconstructions have included 1825 pattern forage caps, but Ebenezer Heath specifically stated that the Grays' caps were made of sealskin. Once again trade advertisements show that sealskin hunting caps were readily available in New Orleans at this time, and the very typical example illustrated here is taken from an 1836 painting of a turkey shoot by Charles Deas.

A variety of weapons were used, including pistols and the inevitable butcher knives, but most of the Grays were armed with rifles provided by their sponsors – probably the same 1817 pattern Common Rifle issued to Bullock's and Winn's companies. Rifles were normally carried in protective cases on the frontier, and one of Pearson's company who survived

Sealskin hunting cap of the style favored by the New Orleans Grays – see Plate B. After an exactly contemporary 1836 painting of a winter turkey shoot, by Charles Deas.

the fight at Julian's Rancho near San Patricio recalled that "The first volley wounded Spence and Hufty; the second volley grazed Baron Von Bunsen on top of his head. The last I saw of him alive was his endeavouring to remove the cover from his rifle, the next, dead, and his body horribly mutilated."

C: REGULARS AT SAN JACINTO, 1836
One of the General Council's first acts had been to send agents to New Orleans to purchase clothing and other supplies. For the most part they simply acquired whatever was available on the open market; supplies sent from New Orleans in January 1836 included 2,012 pairs of brogans or work boots, 366 jackets and pantaloons, 570 pairs of socks and 846 shirts. How much of this actually reached Texas is a different matter; a quantity was certainly lost by shipwreck, and a desperate shortage of clothing and shoes was complained of throughout the campaign. Valentine Bennett, a veteran of Bexar and perhaps of San Jacinto as well, famously declared long after the Texan Revolution that "Rags were our uniform, Sire! Nine out of ten of them was in rags. And it was a fighting uniform!"

C1: Private, 1st Regiment of Infantry
This soldier of the 1st Infantry is wearing a "gray" jeancloth work jacket and pants procured in New Orleans by Thomas McKinney. Jeancloth, a twilled material with a wool weft and cotton warp, was generally dyed gray, but very quickly faded or rather oxidized to a brownish shade or a yellowish butternut. It was light and comfortable, although one North Carolina soldier serving in the Civil War reckoned that

Gentleman in good quality clothing, after a sketch by William Caleb Bingham, Missouri, 1840s. This provides a good illustration of the sort of clothing worn by some of the Texian leaders. Sam Houston was certainly seen wearing a very shabby black frock-coat like this one at San Jacinto, but otherwise more practical outdoor clothing was preferred.

in the field a jacket would last about three months, but that pants wore out in one – so it is easy to understand Bennett's contention that the Texians at San Jacinto were in rags. This soldier has been fortunate enough to get one of the new pairs of brogans also shipped by McKinney, but until they are properly broken in he prefers to march barefoot. Bare feet were not at all unusual in the army during the Revolution, and Fannin complained at one point that even the corporal mounting the guard outside his quarters was barefoot.

C2: Major John Allen, 1st Infantry

Second-in-command of the 1st Infantry at San Jacinto was Captain and acting Major John M.Allen, a Kentucky-born mercenary and adventurer who had fought alongside Lord Byron in Greece before moving to Texas in 1830, and signing on with General Mexia for the abortive expedition to Tampico in November 1835. After Mexia's defeat he and Lieutenant Francis Thornton enlisted the survivors into the first company of regulars "that ever marched to the tap of a drum under the provisional government of Texas."

Other than a stray reference to the company as the "Tampico Blues" there is no information on any uniforms

that may have been worn by Allen and his original gang of filibusters. A portrait miniature of Allen does reveal a blue double-breasted coat with gold epaulettes and a high collar encrusted with gold lace, but it is impossible to attribute it to a particular unit. On the other hand at least two other senior Texian officers at San Jacinto – Ed Burleson of the 1st Texas Volunteers and Sidney Sherman of the 2nd – were separately described by eyewitnesses as wearing blue round jackets, which in Burleson's case at least was of homespun jeancloth.

Discharged from the army on 2 December 1836, Allen eventually settled in Galveston where he was elected mayor, and in the crisis of 1842 raised and commanded the Galveston Invincibles, which served as Company D of Davis' regiment on the Nueces. After the annexation of Texas he was appointed US marshal for the Eastern District of Texas, but died on 12 February 1847.

C3: Deserter, US 7th Infantry

The ranks of the Texian army at San Jacinto were swelled by a surprising number of deserters from the US Army, who for the most part openly wore their old uniforms (though our subject has "lost" his US cartridge box belt plate.) One officer sent to reclaim them after the fighting estimated that there were upwards of 200 of them, all readily identified by their uniforms (but few, if any, were inclined to return with him.) Some of the deserters may have worn the sky-blue kersey fatigue uniform and leather "hog-killer" cap officially adopted in 1833, but this clothing took some time to reach the frontier. The evidence clearly shows that the 7th Infantry, stationed at Fort Jessup and along the Texian border, were actually still wearing out the older gray fatigue uniform when the Texas Revolution began. Quartermaster Department correspondence reveals that old pattern fatigue uniforms (and 1825 pattern forage caps) were certainly issued to the regiment in the summer of 1834. Since authority to sell off any surplus stocks of the old pattern was not given to a number of widely scattered army posts until late 1835, it is reasonable to conclude that the gray uniform had again been issued to the 7th earlier that summer. Indeed, as late as October 1838 an official inspection report on troops at Buffalo Barracks revealed that many were still "clad in old fatigue dresses, much patched."

D: REGULAR INFANTRY, 1836–41

D1: Private, 1st Regiment of Infantry, 1836

Notwithstanding a perennial shortage of hard cash, considerable efforts were made by Texan purchasing agents to provide adequate supplies of clothing and equipment for the army. Although the provisional government resolved in March 1836 to order 2,000 uniform "gray suits," the actual shipping manifests show that Texan agents such as Thomas Toby & Brother were still simply picking up whatever was available ready-made on the open market rather than placing orders with manufacturers for new clothing.

In July, Toby sent a suspiciously complete set of accoutrements which looks as if it might have been a US Government contract that somehow went astray, since it comprised 500 cartridge boxes, bayonet belts and scabbards, 500 leather caps, 500 haversacks (knapsacks?), 500 pint tin cups and 596 canteens. On the other hand, the clothing which accompanied these accoutrements amounted to only 456 pairs of trousers, of which 288 were of white cotton, 24 (white?) duck and 144 striped twill. A subsequent shipment in September was even more mixed, and included 400 pairs of brogans, 120 pairs of brown linen trousers and 240 of blue, but only 194 brown jackets – although a further 360 mainly blue (jeans) trousers were promised. Shirts supplied at this time were a mixture of red flannel and Russia duck.

This reconstruction of a soldier of the 1st Infantry, re-equipped after San Jacinto, is based on the Toby shipments. He wears a brown/butternut jeans jacket and trousers of contrasting shades, with US accoutrements and a leather "hog-killer" – the US 1833 pattern forage cap.

D2: Private, 1st Regiment of Infantry, 1840

Over the next few years the position gradually improved. After September 1836 the jeans work clothing was militarized to a degree by the addition of brass buttons purchased from Scovills of Waterbury, Connecticut, bearing a large star surrounded by the inscription REPUBLIC OF TEXAS. While 208 sealskin hunting caps of the kind earlier worn by the New Orleans Grays were acquired in February 1837, no fewer than 1,093 "forage caps" – presumably the same US 1833 pattern as provided by Thomas Toby – were bought on 5 April, which more than sufficed for all the regular soldiers still serving at that time. The actual provision of clothing also improved; in June 1838 $10,080-worth of cloth was bought from S.W.Tibbutts and made up into uniforms under the supervision of Colonel Sidney Sherman. Unfortunately there is little to indicate the form of this new clothing; but on 23 May 1839 the secretary of war, A.S.Johnston, published for the first time a set of uniform regulations, which probably for the most part codified existing practice rather than introducing much in the way of innovation.

This soldier of the "Frontier Regiment" wears the prescribed fatigue or ordinary working dress, which differed little if at all from that worn previously: a single-breasted gray cloth jacket with a single row of nine front buttons, and plain gray trousers. Note the black tape trim around the shoulder straps and top, bottom and front edges of the collar, and in two loops set on the collar (as on Plate C3). On 15 October 1839 substantial orders for clothing, including 560 fatigue jackets and 1,120 pairs of fatigue pants, were placed with William R.Burke of New York. Prior to shipping these were approved by US Government inspectors, so presumably they were made of gray wool kersey rather than the jeancloth worn previously. In November of the same year 840 dark blue forage caps (560 with white buttons for infantry, and 280 with gilt buttons for cavalry) were also ordered from Gilbert Cleland of New York, and approved by US inspectors, so were presumably exactly the same as the new 1839 pattern forage cap just adopted by the US Army. The 2,240 pairs of laced bootees (4 pairs apiece for the infantry) ordered from John Malseed of Philadelphia were certainly required to be "equal in every respect" to those supplied to the US Army, as were the wooden canteens of 1½ quart capacity ordered from Henry Lutz.

The "new" 1st Infantry were equipped with 1816 pattern Springfield muskets, purchased from George W.Tryon & Sons

Teamster, after a sketch by George Caleb Bingham, Missouri, 1840s. Note the very high waist of the trousers. The very creased appearance of the jacket and trousers indicates that they are made of light jeancloth.

of Philadelphia. In November 1839 orders were placed with William Cressman of the same city for 560 sets of accoutrements, decorated with white metal plates bearing a raised five-point star. The exact form of these accoutrements is a little uncertain since in addition to the essential cartridge boxes and slings, both bayonet belts and waist belts were ordered, the cartridge and bayonet belts both to have plates. Perhaps an initial order for cross belts was modified when it was learnt that US regulars were changing to waist belts.

D3: First Sergeant in full dress

When Johnston expanded the old 1st Infantry to encompass the whole of the regular army he also provided it with a dress uniform, based predictably enough on that worn by the US Army. The dark blue tail-coat was single-breasted with one row of ten front buttons, and a standing collar which was supposed to be closed in front with hooks and eyes. There was to be a single 4-in. loop of white lace on each side of the collar, with a button at the outer end. There were also to be shoulder cords of white worsted, four buttons round the cuff, and a white worsted star at the end of each skirt. Sergeants

were distinguished by three chevrons on the right arm above the elbow, point up, the company first sergeant being further distinguished by a straight line joining the ends of the lower chevron, and a red worsted sash round his waist. Corporals had the customary two chevrons, but wore them below the elbow. Other than the headgear, the principal difference between this dress uniform and that worn by the US Army was that the winter trousers were of dark blue rather than sky blue cloth, with an inch-wide (25mm) white worsted stripe down the outside seam. Plain white cotton drilling trousers were to be worn in summer.

The regulations also prescribed a bell-topped dress cap or shako, with a rayed plate bearing a five-point star, and the usual cords and chin scales. However, although these shakos were used by both regular and militia units in the USA, there are no references to either the caps or the plates in the otherwise comprehensive purchase orders for clothing, inspectors' certificates, shipping manifests or stores inventories. Infantry dress caps only appear, paradoxically enough, in inventories of stores held in the Galveston Navy Yard – but these are almost certainly old US Army ones acquired along with surplus Marine uniforms.

As with the fatigue uniforms, contracts for the blues were placed with William Burke in October. Interestingly the order was actually for 480 blue infantry coats for privates, 40 for corporals and 40 for sergeants and regimental staff. At first

sight this might suggest that – as in some other armies – the NCOs' uniforms were of superior quality, were it not for the fact that all 560 pairs of trousers accompanying the coats were of the same quality. The distinction must presumably have lain in the NCOs' coats having their stripes directly applied at the factory. If so, the fact that no such distinction was made to the fatigue jackets may possibly indicate that no rank badges were worn on the grays.

E: REGULAR OFFICERS, 1839–41
E1: Colonel William Gordon Cooke
Cooke had perhaps the most distinguished career of all Texas officers. Born in 1808 in Fredericksburg, Virginia, he was originally trained as a druggist. As a captain of the New Orleans Grays he took a prominent part in the storming of Bexar in December 1835, and afterwards marched with Grant to Refugio as commander of the San Antonio Grays. There he enlisted as a permanent volunteer, and was shortly afterwards sent by Fannin to Washington-on-the-Brazos, thus escaping the massacre of his command at Goliad. Cooke served on Houston's staff at San Jacinto, and then as the Republic's first secretary of war from November 1836 to July 1837. In October 1838 he rejoined the army as quartermaster general; took part in the Council House Fight; and was appointed colonel of the 1st Regiment of Infantry on 18 August 1840. In the following year he took a prominent role in the Santa Fe débâcle, and after his release served under Edward Burleson in operations against General Woll, being wounded in the fight at Arroyo Hondo on 22 September 1842. On 25 October he was reappointed quartermaster general and took part in the Somervell expedition, but had more sense than to continue on to Mier. Next he sailed with the Texas Navy to Yucatan, and after his return to Galveston in July 1843 became adjutant general of the Texas Militia. He again served as secretary of war from December 1844 until annexation, and as adjutant general of the state of Texas from 27 April 1846 until his death from tuberculosis on 24 December 1847.

Cooke is depicted here wearing the double-breasted frock-coat as prescribed for staff officers in 1839. The black velvet shoulder straps bear gold borders and a silver star between two sets of three crossed arrows. Field officers wore their buttons evenly spaced, major-generals in threes and brigadier-generals in pairs; both grades were also to wear red silk sashes instead of the yellow/buff staff type shown here. For general officers the shoulder straps bore three or two stars only, within broader gold borders; their dress coat was to have both epaulettes and a gold aiguillette. Trousers for general and staff officers alike were to be of dark blue cloth in winter, with an inch-wide buff stripe on the outer seam, and of plain white linen in summer. The sword belt was of black patent leather, the gilt plate bearing the star between branches of live oak.
E2: Ordnance officer
When all the regulars were consolidated into an expanded 1st Regiment of Infantry, the few remaining officers and men of the old 1st Artillery were redesignated as Ordnance

Raftsman, Missouri, sometime before 1847, after a sketch by George Caleb Bingham. The hat appears to be straw, the trousers jeancloth; and note the shoulder detail of the full shirt-sleeves.

Rank badges on shoulder straps as prescribed in 1839; see Plate E. The straps were to be of black velvet edged with gold or silver braid according to button color. The various devices were to be of the opposite color, i.e. silver if the edging was gold. (Left to right, top to bottom) major-general, brigadier-general; colonel, lieutenant-colonel; major, captain; first lieutenant, second lieutenant.

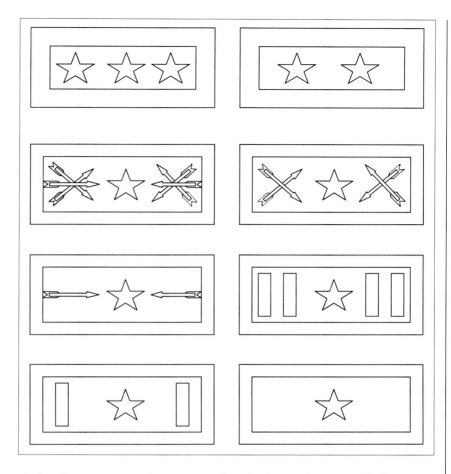

Detachments. At the same time their officers were prescribed this dress uniform – though whether they ever wore it is perhaps a moot point. The coat lining visible at the tails was buff, and there was a half-inch buff stripe down the trouser outseam. In full dress field officers were supposed to have an epaulette on both shoulders, captains a single epaulette on the right and lieutenants one on the left. This uniform at least must have been a completely new one, since the regulations expressly stated that the buttons (bearing a star above crossed cannon) were to be "as at present adopted," which clearly suggests that the rest of it was not. The regulations also referred to a dress cap which was to be the same as that worn by the infantry, except for an orange pom-pon; but as these caps were seemingly never actually adopted, this field officer wears the ubiquitous forage cap.

E3: Captain of infantry

According to the 1839 regulations the undress uniform for both infantry and ordnance officers comprised a single-breasted dark blue frock coat with a single row of ten buttons – here silver for infantry. The cuff was plain, with three small buttons on the rear. Rank was indicated by shoulder straps which resembled those used by the US Army, although the actual insignia were rather different: here, silver borders enclosing a gold star between two pairs of gold captain's bars. In winter trousers were to be of dark blue cloth with an inch-wide white stripe for dress, and a white cassimere cord for undress; the usual plain white linen

trousers were allowed to be worn in summer. The forage cap was of the same style as worn by the enlisted men, without an integral neck flap but with an oiled silk cover for bad weather. Belts were of black patent leather and the clasp "according to pattern" – just what pattern this might have been does not appear, but the reference to a clasp rather than a plate indicates that it was probably a two-piece design featuring a star on the "spoon."

F: THE CAVALRY

F1: Colonel Lysander Wells, 1840

Described in a newspaper report at the time as "elegantly uniformed," Colonel Wells was almost certainly wearing the full 1839 dress uniform as prescribed for cavalry officers when he took part in the "Council House Fight" against Comanches in San Antonio on 15 March 1840. The dark blue coat was to be single-breasted, with three rows of buttons on the front – nine functional ones down the centre and 11 decorative ones in each side row. The skirts were to be very short, no more than 4ins in length. The collar was edged top and front with gold cord, and bore five oakleaf-and-acorn sprigs; the plain cuffs had four buttons around the top and three small buttons up the rear seam; and Colonel Wells wears epaulettes with gilt brass scale straps and crescents and bullion fringes. The trousers were also to be dark blue with a 1½-in. buff stripe on the outseam, but interestingly had a fly front rather than the fall front worn by the infantry.

The helmet – described very particularly in the regulations as being "according to pattern, with a white horse hair plume, the Colonel to be designed by a tuft of red horse hair in the front of his plume" – seems to have been identical to the old US 1812 pattern helmet. This was of black leather with a 6-in. deep skull and a flowing white horsehair crest (not "plume") set into the 3-in. high comb which surmounted it. The only difference appears to be that the US white metal plate, featuring a cavalryman within an oval, was to be replaced by a gilt rayed plate with a star in the centre. However, although Colonel Wells is dashingly depicted wearing this helmet, there is once again no evidence that they were actually adopted by the army, since like the prescribed infantry dress caps they do not appear in any purchase orders, inspectors' reports, shipping manifests or other stores inventories.

Unsurprisingly a sword is the only weapon mentioned for officers in the 1839 regulations, but Wells was also armed at the Council House Fight with a new Colt's 1836 Paterson model revolver in 0.36in calibre – which made a decidedly inauspicious debut by jamming when a Comanche warrior jumped up behind him. Happily Wells still succeeded in dispatching his assailant, only to be fatally wounded in a duel with Captain William Redd of the 1st Infantry on 9 May. Redd, whom he had quite unjustly accused of cowardice, was killed outright.

F2: Trooper in service dress, 1840

When William B. Travis set about raising the original Corps of Cavalry in December 1835 he proposed that they should be armed with "broadswords," rifles and shotguns, and dressed in "a suit of cadet grey cloth coats, [with] yellow bullet buttons, and pantaloons for winter, and two suits of grey cottonade roundabouts and pantaloons for summer, and fur caps, black cloth stocks and cowhide boots." While it is unlikely that any of his men who died with him at the Alamo were wearing this uniform, it does seem probable that (with the likely exception of the fur caps), it was afterwards worn by the rump of the regiment which soldiered on as the 1st Dragoons. At any rate, while the 1839 regulations prescribed a dark blue dress coat (red for trumpeters) and trousers, with brass shoulder scales and a maned helmet, the ordinary service dress consisted of a cadet gray jacket and trousers with the ubiquitous forage cap, which suggests a certain continuity with the uniform devised by Travis back in 1835. Note that the collar is only edged with black tape and bears no buttonhole loops, and that the long black-edged shoulder strap buttons to the collar itself. Plain white cotton drilling jackets and trousers were also authorized for wear in the summer.

All belts and pouches were to be of black leather and the regulations described each trooper as being armed with a saber, carbine and pistol "According to pattern in the Ordnance Department." The swords – as ordered in February 1840 – were the US 1833 pattern made by N.P. Ames of Springfield, Massachusetts; judging by other evidence the pistols also conformed to current US patterns. The carbines, however, present a problem; all that is known with any certainty is that 250 Jenks carbines were delivered in April 1841. This was a rather curious breechloader which performed well in tests, despite perennial problems of fouling, but suffered from the fact that it had to be loaded with loose powder and ball. It also obviously arrived too late, although there are references to its use in the following year

by both the Galveston Hussars and the Galveston Fusiliers. It is possible that the cavalry troopers at the Council House Fight and Plum Creek may have been armed with the US Army's Hall breechloader, but there is no real evidence on this point, and they may in fact still have been armed with the rifles and double-barreled shotguns advocated by Travis.

F3: Officer in service dress

For ordinary undress cavalry officers were prescribed the usual forage cap and a dark blue cloth coat "cut after the fashion of citizen's coat," with falling collar and two rows of buttons, which could be worn on all duties when full dress was not required. At stables and on active duty, however, they were specifically permitted to wear shell jackets of the same pattern and color as worn by the men, i.e. "cadet grey," trimmed with black braid in winter and white drilling in summer. This officer wears his winter jacket open to reveal the double-breasted buff vest or "weskit." Officers were also allowed to wear overalls, with concealed buttons up the outside, but this captain wears a pair of civilian jeancloth trousers tucked into the regulation high boots. Like Colonel Wells, he has a privately purchased Colt's Paterson revolver.

G: VOLUNTEERS, 1842

The five companies of infantry and one of artillery assembled for the Santa Fe expedition in 1841 were kitted out before their departure with surplus regular army uniforms, which chiefly included 233 blue cavalry coats and a fairly miscellaneous mixture of cavalry fatigue jackets and trousers. What remained in the stores was afterwards turned over for the use of the militia; but on 30 April in the following year Jacob Snively, the acting quartermaster and commissary, recovered it for issue to the volunteers assembling under Davis on the Nueces. This clothing included 33 blue cavalry jackets, 132 blue infantry jackets, 39 pairs of blue trousers, 15 infantry gray jackets and 52 pairs of gray trousers, 13 "cadet grey" cavalry jackets and 43 pairs of matching trousers, 79 white drill jackets, 171 fly-fronted white drill cavalry trousers, and 33 pairs of fall-fronted infantry drill trousers.

G1: Trooper, Galveston Hussars

Although no issue records survive, the Galveston Hussars were evidently regarded as an elite unit; they were equipped with some of the Jenks carbines, and so probably had the pick of the uniforms as well – hence the blue cavalry jacket and trousers illustrated here. Note the yellow lace framing the otherwise plain collar, brass shoulder loops for attaching the shoulder scales of dress uniform, and the same button arrangement as on Plate F1. While this trooper, loading his carbine with a US Rifleman's powder flask, has an old forage cap, none of these actually appear in the lists of stores turned over to Snively, and hats may have predominated.

G2: Galveston Coast Guard

Another unit raised in response to the renewed threat from Mexico was the Galveston Coast Guards, some of whom were embarked with the Galveston Fusiliers as marines on board the steamer Lafitte. According to a volunteer named Bollaert, they were uniformly dressed in red wool shirts, white trousers and straw hats, and were armed with the customary assortment of firearms, butcher knives and hatchets. This particular individual has an 1817 pattern Common Rifle.

Bollaert was less forthcoming about the Galveston Fusiliers, saying only that they were "habited in modest

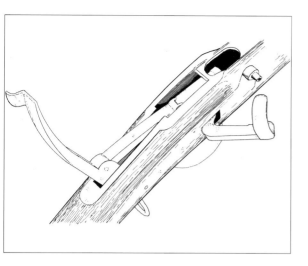

The loading mechanism of the Jenks carbine; see Plate G. Pulling the top lever up and forward drew back a bolt which exposed the breech. Early models were fitted with flintlocks, but those supplied to the Texians were of this later sidehammer percussion model. Not surprisingly, one Texian volunteer described them as "queer-looking".

uniforms." These may simply have been gray jeancloth work jackets and pants, but as Bollaert also noted that they were armed with "a rather queer looking breech loading rifle" – the Jenks – it is possible that the "modest uniforms" may have been gray fatigue jackets and trousers drawn from the militia stores.

G3: Texas Ranger

This Ranger is based in part on an 1834 portrait of Colonel Henry Dodge of the US 1st Dragoons, and a number of contemporary descriptions. Under his hunting shirt he wears a gray fatigue jacket and trousers drawn from the militia stores, as are his old leather forage cap and cavalry belt; the jacket is worn partly open at the neck over a red shirt and black bandana. Many of the Rangers also improvised buckskin leggings for protection against the chapparal. Pistols and Colt's revolvers were carried by all who cared to have them, while rifles were *de rigueur*. At Mier in 1842 Fisher's unruly volunteers initially enjoyed a considerable tactical advantage from being armed with percussion weapons which performed far better than Mexican flintlocks in the prevailing bad weather.

H: THE NAVY

Almost from the very outbreak of the Revolution, Texas had a navy. Because of the great distances involved and the considerable numbers of rivers to be crossed on the overland routes, so far as possible supplies and recruits were shipped by sea from New Orleans to Velasco or one of the other small ports along the Texas coast. The schooners and steamers employed in this work obviously needed to be protected; the Texian Council first commissioned privateers, and then its own very aggressive navy. Moribund after the Revolution, it was quite literally relaunched by Lamar and – oddly enough – fought its biggest sea battle off Campeche in 1841 while under contract to the rebel

Mexican state of Yucatan. This was the action subsequently immortalized as the "sea fight" engraving on the cylinder of Colt's famous 1851 model Navy revolver.

H1: Commodore Edwin Moore

Born in 1810 in Alexandria, Virginia, Edwin Moore entered the US Navy in 1825; he was serving as a lieutenant on board the USS *Boston* in July 1839 when he resigned to become commander of the Texas Navy. A conscientious officer, he ensured that his men were well looked after, co-operated effectively with the Federalist rebels in the Yucatan, and gained that useful victory over the Mexican Navy off Campeche. Houston, who had tried on the grounds of economy to stop him sailing for Yucatan, had him court-martialed on his return for disobedience, contumacy, mutiny, piracy and murder. Notwithstanding this impressive indictment, Moore was found not guilty, although it took until 1857 to recover his back pay.

On 13 March 1839 the Navy Department published a commendably brief set of uniform regulations that were restricted to describing the dress of commissioned and warrant officers – although stores inventories reveal the near-universal blue jackets and duck trousers for ordinary seamen. In broad outline British and American practice was followed, and the most common sea-going rig for officers appears to have been a dark blue roundabout and peaked cap. Trousers could be "grey cloth, brown drilling, yellow or blue nankeen… also black or figured vests, of any colour except red." With refreshing simplicity, officers were also allowed as undress "a citizen's blue cloth dress coat, cut after the fashion prevailing at the day, with the requisite number of buttons as in full dress, and the straps on the shoulders for those who are entitled to wear epaulettes."

H2: Sergeant of Marines dress uniform

There is no evidence that the navy included any officers of Marines, and there is certainly no mention of them in the naval dress regulations. Nor was a uniform prescribed for the rank and file; but when the neighboring US Marine Corps changed its grass green dress uniforms for blue ones in 1839, surplus stocks of the old pattern were acquired by Texian purchasing agents and "Texanized" simply by changing the buttons. The piping, lace button loops, rank badges and wool epaulettes are yellow/buff. Gray trousers, with a buff stripe down the outside seam for NCOs, were also obtained from the same source, as apparently were the leather dress caps or shakos earlier turned over to the US Marines by the Army back in 1834. Stores inventories for the Navy Yard at Galveston show a small stock of these caps, but they were evidently not taken on board ship, presumably because they took up too much valuable storage space. Instead the quite distinctive US Marine forage caps were worn with the dress coats: these had a green band and top and a yellow/buff crown.

H3: Marine shore landing rig

On board ship the small detachments of Texian marines normally wore ordinary seamen's slop clothing – just as they did in most other navies – but for shore duties and landing parties they had infantry-style gray fatigue jackets and trousers, together with dark blue infantry forage caps. In hot weather white jackets and trousers could also be issued. Landing parties tended to be heavily armed, and this man has a Colt's revolving carbine.

INDEX

Figures in **bold** refer to illustrations.